CW01192426

LINES NORTH OF STOKE

to Crewe, Congleton and Leek

Adrian Hartless

Series editor Vic Mitchell

MP Middleton Press

Front cover: Electrification, including re-signalling, was implemented at Stoke before the elimination of steam. On 29th October 1966, class 2MT 2-6-2T no. 41204 from Stockport shed worked a brake van tour for the Railway Correspondence & Travel Society to Cheadle and return, and then to Caldon Low and return. Here, it awaits the start. Modernisation did not disguise the lines of the NSR's overall roof and offices. Another change was the removal of the down through line; its formation was lifted in 1965 and the space was used for overhead line electrification masts. (Colour-Rail)

Published April 2019

ISBN 978 1 910356 29 6

© Middleton Press Ltd, 2019

Production editor & Cover design Deborah Esher
Production & design Cassandra Morgan

Published by
    Middleton Press Ltd
    Easebourne Lane
    Midhurst
    West Sussex
    GU29 9AZ
Tel: 01730 813169
Email: info@middletonpress.co.uk
www.middletonpress.co.uk

Printed and bound by CPI Group (UK) Ltd, Croydon, CR0 4YY

CONTENTS

1. Leek – Stoke – Crewe   1-76   3. Etruria – Burslem – Congleton   80-111
2. Sandbach Route   77-79   4. Biddulph Route   112-120

INDEX

65	Alsager	80	Hanley	99	Newchapel & Goldenhill
114	Biddulph	78	Hassall Green		
115	Black Bull	59	Kidsgrove	96	Pitts Hill
20	Bucknall & Northwood		(formerly Harecastle)	72	Radway Green & Bartholmley
		103	Kidsgrove Liverpool Road		
90	Burslem	101	Kidsgrove Halt	14	Stockton Brook
54	Chatterley	77	Lawton	24	Stoke-on-Trent
87	Cobridge	1	Leek	93	Tunstall
108	Congleton	5	Leek Brook	7	Wall Grange & Longsdon
74	Crewe	49	Longport		
10	Endon	17	Milton	86	Waterloo Road
43	Etruria	105	Mow Cop & Scholar Green	79	Wheelock & Sandbach
22	Fenton Manor				
118	Ford Green & Smallthorne				

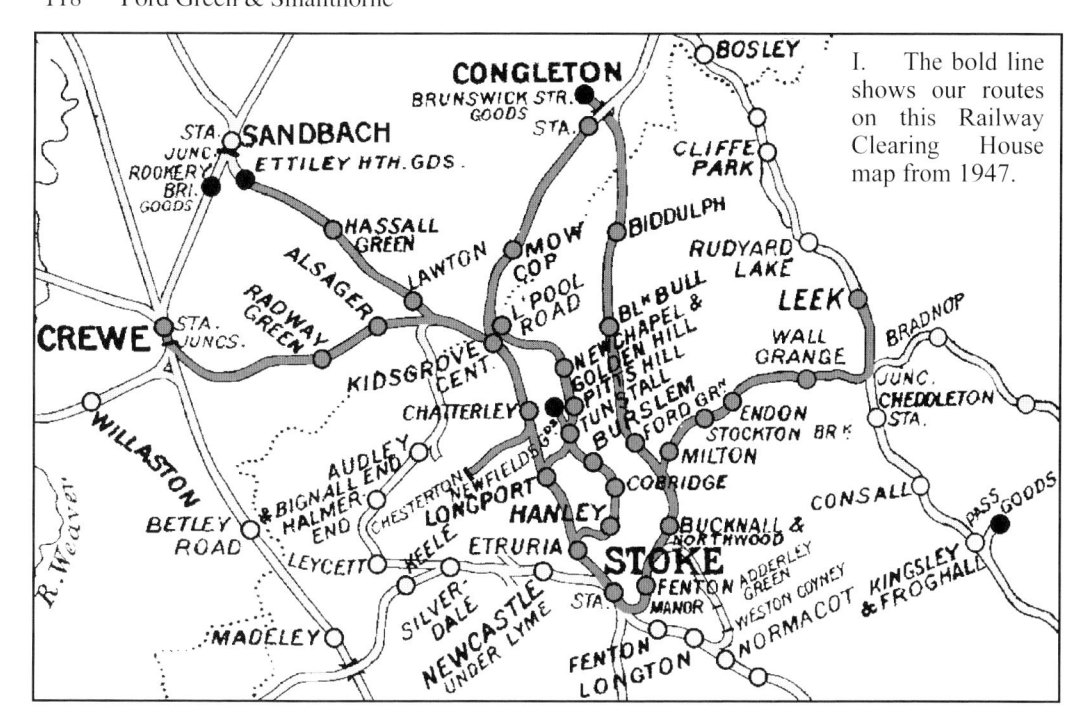

I. The bold line shows our routes on this Railway Clearing House map from 1947.

ACKNOWLEDGEMENTS

    This album is dedicated to the memory of my father-in-law, John 'Jack' Moore (1904-81). His working life included time as a ganger on the lines covered herein and, apart from Army service, he spent all his days in Stoke-on-Trent, ultimately at Bucknall. Thanks are due to Nick Allsop for sharing his knowledge of North Staffs Railway signalling and to Chris Knight at North Staffs Rly Co (1978) Ltd Museum, and also to C.M.Howard and N.Langridge.

GEOGRAPHICAL SETTING

The River Trent rises on moorland near Biddulph and flows south through Stoke. It is paralleled to the east by the River Churnet on which stands the town of Leek. To their north the River Dane flows westward from the Pennines onto the Cheshire Plain. The locality is part of Staffordshire except for the north west, which is in Cheshire.

The predominant eco-geological feature is the band of Etruria Marl extending from south of Stoke to north of Tunstall, which gave rise to the pottery industry on which the historic prosperity of North Staffordshire was based. Immediately to the west, underlying the valley of Fowlea Brook, a tributary of the Trent, are coal and ironstone measures which led to rapid industrialisation in the 18th Century. Like the china clay these have been economically exhausted. The remainder of North Staffs is on millstone grit, which rises to over 1,650ft north of Leek. Cheshire lies to the west of a geological fault line and is gentler country, suited to dairy farming and underlain by sandstone.

The maps are to the scale of 6ins to 1 mile, with north at the top, and using the revisions of the early 1920s unless otherwise stated.

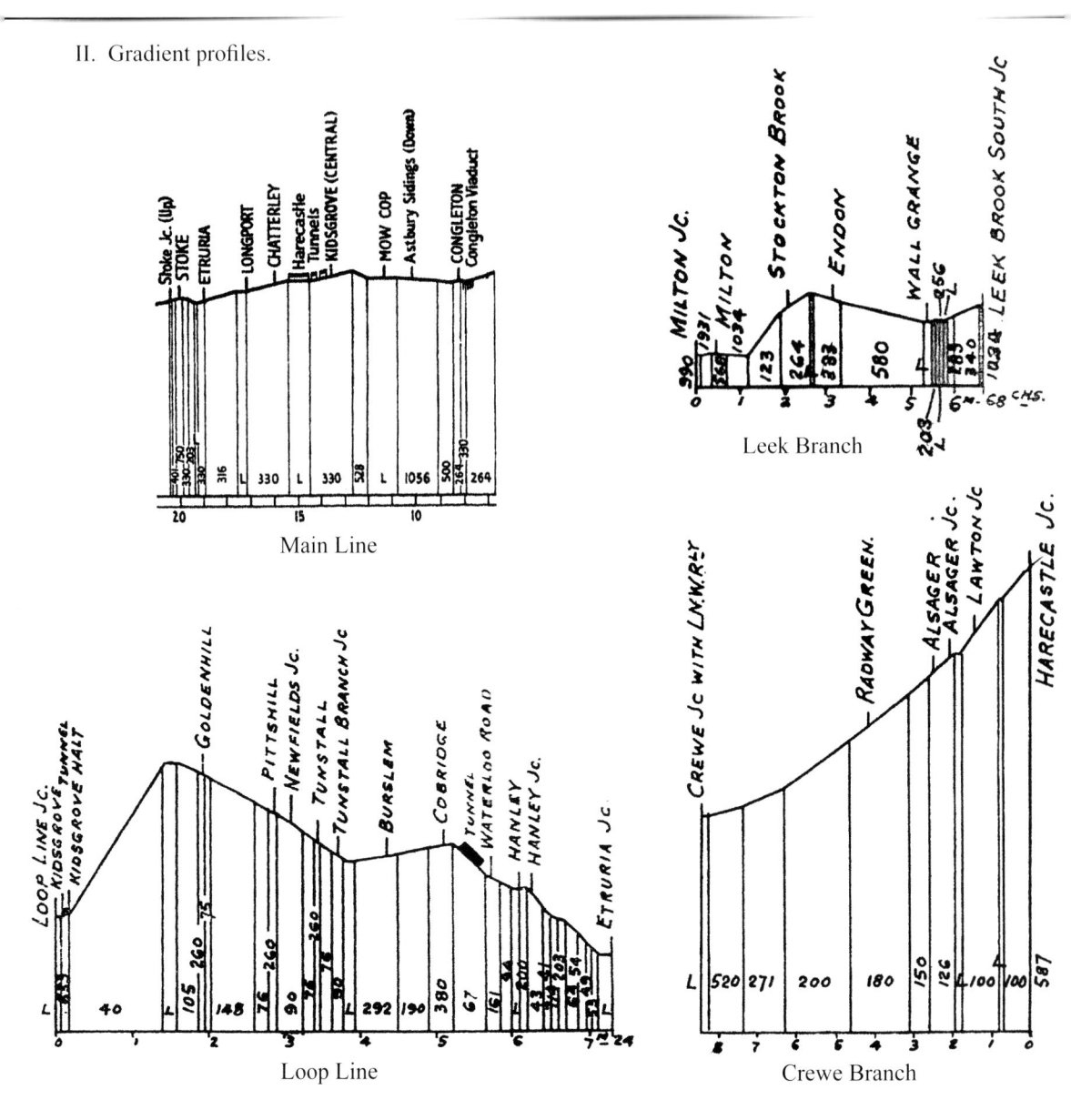

II. Gradient profiles.

Sandbach Branch

Biddulph Valley Branch

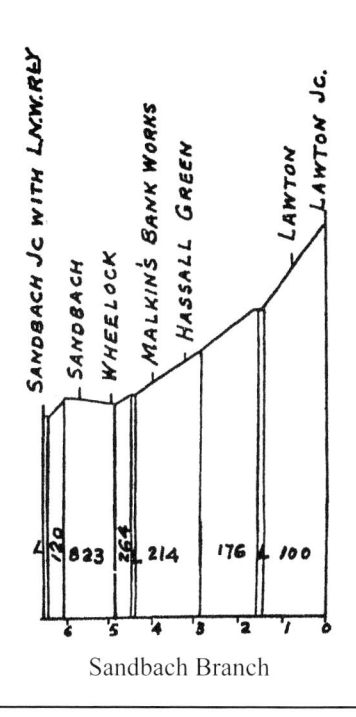

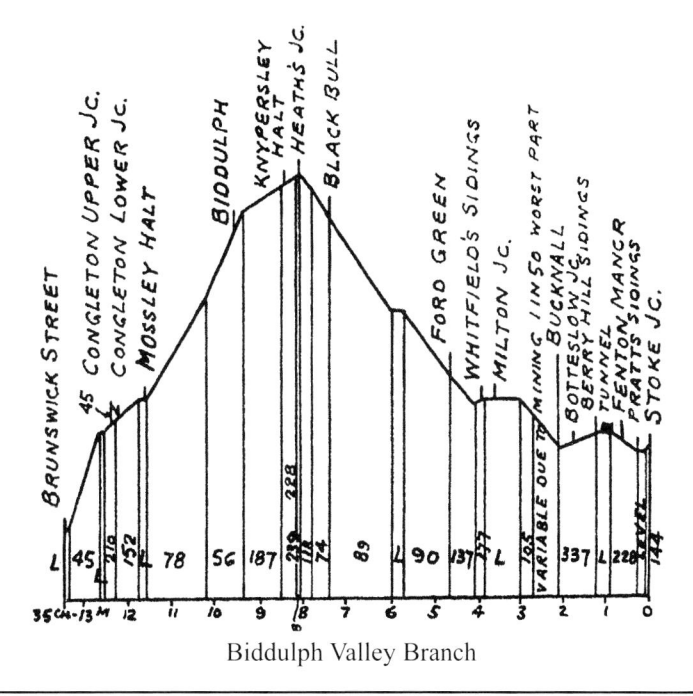

HISTORICAL BACKGROUND

All the lines in this album were built by the North Staffordshire Railway (NSR), which had its headquarters at Stoke Station and remained proudly independent until vested into the London Midland & Scottish Railway from 1st January 1923. The English and Welsh lines of the LMS in turn became the London Midland Region of the nationalised British Railways (BR) from 1st January 1948.

The main lines of the NSR were authorised by a single Act of Parliament of 26th June 1846, and opened within a short space of time from one another, as follows:
Stoke – Norton Bridge 17th April 1848;
Stoke – Uttoxeter 7th August 1848;
Stoke – Congleton/Crewe 9th October 1848;
Congleton – Macclesfield 18th June 1849.

The Sandbach (Wheelock) Branch was the next to open, in 1852, although the passenger service did not commence until 3rd July 1893. The Biddulph Valley line opened in 1859 and was freight only until 1st June 1864; the Leek Branch followed on 1st July 1867. The Potteries Loop Line opened in stages between 1861 and 1875.

The LMS was quick to close unremunerative passenger services, including the Biddulph Valley trains from 11th July 1927 and the Sandbach Branch from 28th July 1930. BR withdrew passenger trains from Leek to Stoke from 7th May 1956, and from the Loop Line from 2nd March 1964. This left the core NSR lines above, which was still the case in 2018.

InterCity West Coast services from London Euston to Manchester Piccadilly were initially operated by Virgin Trains. Virgin won the franchise in March 1997 and was scheduled to continue to operate it until March 2020. As part of the Very High Frequency service introduced in January 2009, Euston to Manchester services were increased to three per hour – two ran via Stoke-on-Trent and one via Crewe.

InterCity Cross Country services from the south of England via Birmingham New Street to Manchester Piccadilly were originally operated by Virgin Cross Country upon privatisation in January 1997. Typically two trains per hour operated, one to Birmingham New Street and one to destinations beyond. The franchise was retendered in November 2007 – Arriva Trains took over and branded services as CrossCountry. In December 2008, a new service pattern was introduced with trains running each hour from Manchester via Stoke to Bournemouth and to Bristol Temple Meads, with some of the latter extending to Exeter St Davids, Paignton or Plymouth.

Central Trains operated services from Northampton to Crewe and Skegness to Manchester Airport (both along the Stoke-on-Trent to Crewe route) upon privatisation in March 1997. Central Trains was remapped in November 2007, with services in this area split between London Midland (LM) and East Midlands Trains (EMT).

LM services were extended to operate between London Euston and Crewe. In December 2017, LM became West Midlands Trains, operating Euston – Crewe under the London Northwestern Railway brand. The Skegness to Manchester Airport service was cut back to Crewe in 2004 and Derby in 2005. The revised Derby to Crewe service passed to EMT, as above.

Hourly local services from Stoke-on-Trent to Manchester Piccadilly were operated by First North Western from privatisation in March 1997 until December 2004. A new, remapped Northern franchise took over at this date, to be replaced by another of the same name in April 2016.

The main line from London Euston through Stoke-on-Trent to Manchester Piccadilly was electrified in 1966. The route from Kidsgrove to Crewe followed in 2003, primarily to allow diverted electric trains to operate during the West Coast Route Modernisation programme. This was ultimately completed in December 2008.

Freight services were the bread and butter of the NSR, but following the loss of their heavy industries leading up to the start of the 21st Century, the Potteries no longer have any regular rail freight traffic. This decline is evidenced by the pictures and captions that follow.

PASSENGER SERVICES

Down trains running on at least five days per weeks are listed below.

Leek-Stoke:

	Weekdays	Sundays
1869	4	3
1899	7	3
1921	12	3
1955	5	0

In the 19th Century, most trains continued north to Rudyard, but latterly some ran on to Rushton, notably on Sundays, in the Summer.

Etruria-Congleton:

	Weekdays	Sundays
1850	6	3
1880	6	3
1910	10	3
1930	17	5
1963	17	11

In the early days, Tunstall was on the main line; it was later renamed Chatterley. The Loop Line station opened on 1 December 1873.

Stoke-Crewe:

	Weekdays	Sundays
1850	5	2
1875	7	2
1901	8	2
1923	10	2
1964	21	5
1999	17	7

In recent years, most trains have run hourly, all stations, from Derby to Crewe. Many of the destinations are mentioned in the captions.

Biddulph Route:

	Weekdays	Sundays
1869	2	0
1899	3	0
1926	2	0

Trains called at all stations from Stoke to Congleton.

June 1869

June 1876

April 1880

July 1899

July 1921

1. Leek - Stoke - Crewe

LEEK

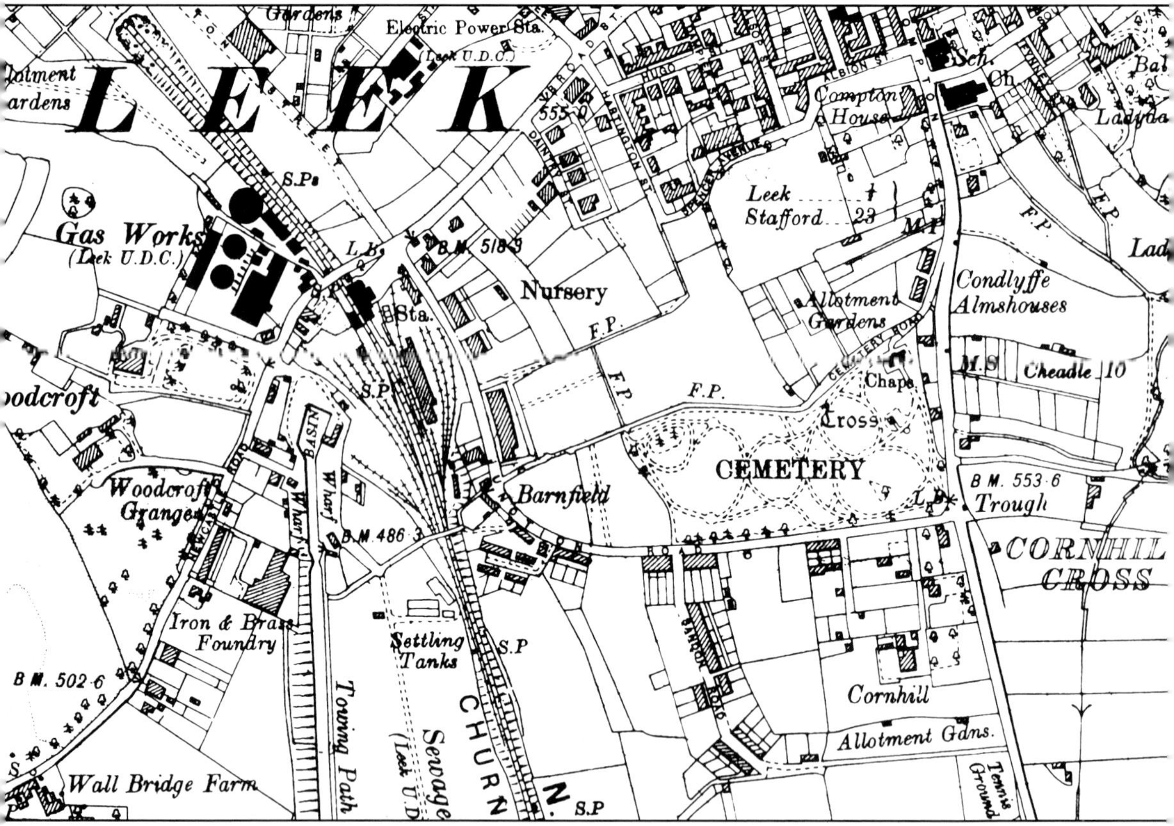

III. The 1925 map shows Leek station south west of the town centre, where the Churnet Valley line was crossed by Newcastle Road, the A53, and close to the canal basin. The station had two through platforms, and a south-facing bay on the east side. South of the station was a substantial goods warehouse with extensive sidings on either side of the running lines with the headshunt south of Barnfield bridge.

January 1955

STOKE-ON-TRENT, LEEK, and RUSHTON

Miles	HOUR	a.m 7	6	—	7	7	—	—	9	—	S 12	Week Days S 12	—	U 3	5	—	6	E 5	E 6	p.m 6	—	Suns. am					pm
—	Stoke-on-Trent .... dep		38			18						55			6			42	10								
1¼	Fenton Manor		42			20						57			8			44	12								
2¾	Bucknall & Northwood A..		47			25						**2**			13			49	17								
5	Milton		52			30						7			18			57	23								
6¾	Stockton Brook B........		57			35						12			23			**2**	28								
7¾	Endon		**0**			38						15			26			5	31								
10	Wall Grange & Longsdon..		5			43						20			31			10	36								
12½	Leek .... arr		12			50						27			38			17	43								
	Leek .... dep	8			46				5		32	30		46			0			58							
14½	Rudyard Lake	11			49				8		35	33		49			3			**1**							
17	Cliffe Park Halt				55						41	39		55			9										
17½	Rushton .... arr	19			58				15		45	43		58			12			10							

Miles	HOUR	a.m 6	6	—	7	8	—	S 12	U 1	—	4	—	Week Days E 5	E 5	—	E 6	S 6	—	E 7	p.m S 8	—	Suns. pm					pm
—	Rushton .... dep		55			10			7		3			39		28	43			59							
½	Cliffe Park Halt		57			12			9		5			41						**1**							
3	Rudyard Lake		**2**			18			14		10			47		35	51			7							
5	Leek .... arr		7			23			19		15			52		40	56			12							
	Leek .... dep	53			57			5					35						40								
7½	Wall Grange & Longsdon..	59			**3**			11					42						46								
9¾	Endon	**4**			8			16					47						51								
10¾	Stockton Brook B........	6			10			18					49						53								
12½	Milton	11			15			23					54						58								
14¾	Bucknall & Northwood A..	15			19			27					58														
16¼	Fenton Manor	20			24			32					**3**						**7**								
17½	Stoke-on-Trent .... arr	25			30			37					7						11								

A Sta. for Hanley (1 mile)
B Sta. for Brown Edge
E Except Saturdays
S Saturdays only
U Wednesdays and Saturdays

Where MINUTES under Hours change to a LOWER figure and DARKER type it indicates NEXT HOUR

1.   This view from Newcastle Road follows the southward course of the Churnet Valley line. The bay platform is on the left with a short rake of passenger stock. Beyond is the goods station and signal box with Barnfield bridge in the distance; this comprises the original arch, and just visible to its right a girder span which was added to accommodate new sidings in the late 19th Century. The deposits on the down line are spilt sand. The picture is undated but appears to be contemporaneous with picture 2. (Railway Station Photographs)

2.   On 27th January 1962, class 4MT 2-6-4T no. 42668, a long serving Stoke locomotive, awaits departure with the 1.35pm to Stoke. This was a 'footex' for the 4th round FA Cup tie between Stoke City, then in Division 2, and Blackburn Rovers of Division 1, which Rovers won 0-1 by a controversial penalty that is remembered to this day. 46 years old Stanley Matthews was in the home team, and drawing large crowds, hence the length of the train. Note the Newcastle Road bridge in the background, the buffer stop of the bay to the right of the loco, and one of the goods sidings beyond. (T.Cooke/Colour-Rail)

3. The station was demolished in 1973, the site was quickly cleared, and a supermarket built. This is the view from the same point as picture 1 on 3rd February 2018. The supermarket is at a 90 degree angle to the railway trackbed. In the right background can be seen the western span of Barnfield bridge. In 2017 the Churnet Valley Railway received planning permission to return to Leek and will locate its replacement station at Barnfield, nowadays called Cornhill West. (A.C.Hartless)

4. The Newcastle Road bridge was retained, including the steps to the down platform on the left. The trackbed was turned into a roadway linking the supermarket building, behind the camera, with the petrol pumps. This approximates to picture 2. (A.C.Hartless)

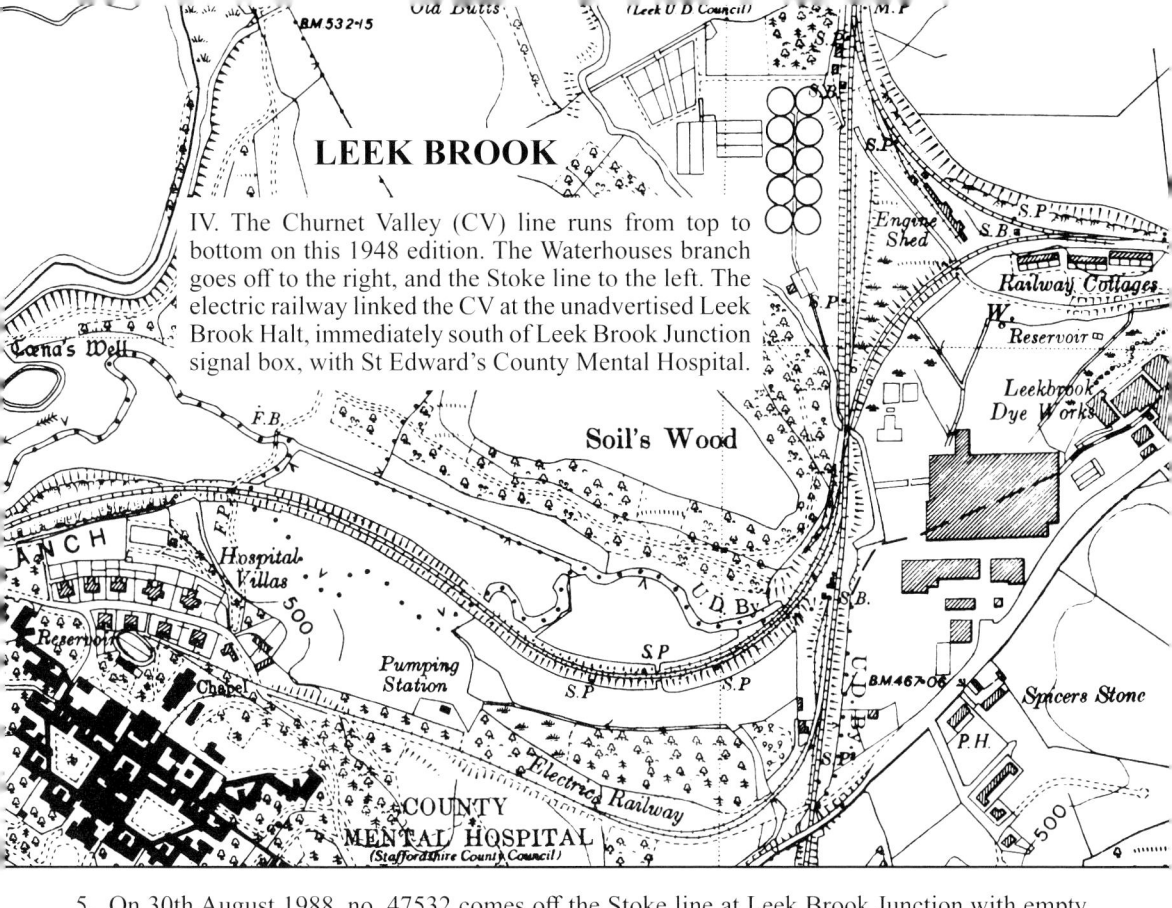

LEEK BROOK

IV. The Churnet Valley (CV) line runs from top to bottom on this 1948 edition. The Waterhouses branch goes off to the right, and the Stoke line to the left. The electric railway linked the CV at the unadvertised Leek Brook Halt, immediately south of Leek Brook Junction signal box, with St Edward's County Mental Hospital.

5. On 30th August 1988, no. 47532 comes off the Stoke line at Leek Brook Junction with empty mineral wagons for Caldon Low Quarry. This was the last day of sand by rail from Oakamoor, the line in the foreground. Until the withdrawal of the Stoke – Leek passenger service there was an unadvertised platform for workmen's use. This was between the up and down Stoke lines, which were subsequently re-aligned, and can be seen in picture 72 of *Uttoxeter to Macclesfield*. The NSR out-sourced much of its signalling infrastructure from the firm of McKenzie & Holland, and the distinctive signalbox here was one of the earliest to be installed on its system, in 1872. It closed in 1989 but happily was not demolished. It was given Grade II listed status in 2008, and the Churnet Valley Railway has restored it to operational use. (North Staffs Rly Co (1978) Ltd Museum coll.)

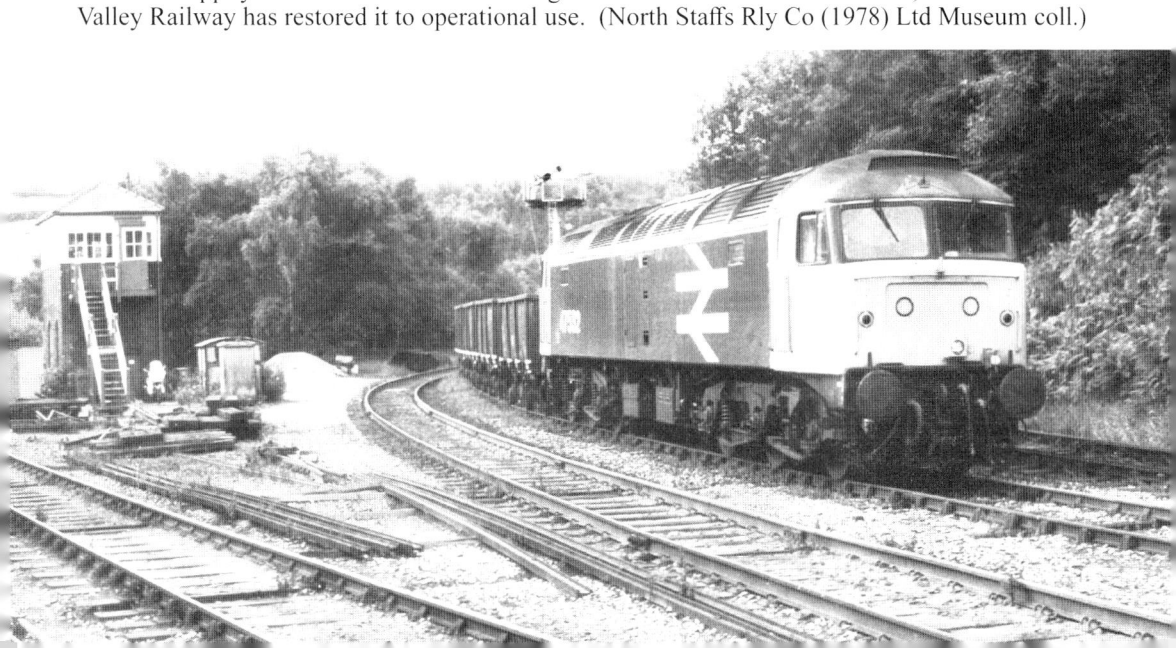

6. The Churnet Valley Railway was already in occupation at Cheddleton before the freight services ended and has subsequently expanded its activities. This is the northward view along the CV route on 3rd February 2018, during the railway's Winter Steam Gala. USATC 2-8-0 no. 6046 has just come off the Caldon Low branch, which can be seen going to the right in the centre background, and is running tender first to Cheddleton. The Oakamoor line also had an unadvertised halt, which CVR has re-established along with a run round loop on the double track formation. The halt re-opened on 25th June 2016, and later in 2018 a waiting shelter was provided. In common with its predecessor there is no public access other than from the train. The electric railway to St Edward's Hospital used the left-hand side of the original platform, and its formation can still be seen. The Stoke line was still in place; its junction, to the rear of the train, is partly obscured by the signaller. It then runs behind the signalbox and the fence to its left. (A.C.Hartless)

> **Further pictures of Leek and Leek Brook Junction can be seen in the** *Uttoxeter to Macclesfield* **and** *Branch Line from Leek* **albums from Middleton Press.**

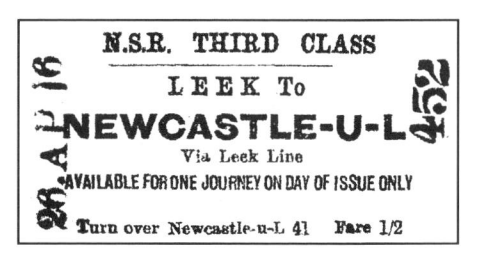

WALL GRANGE & LONGSDON

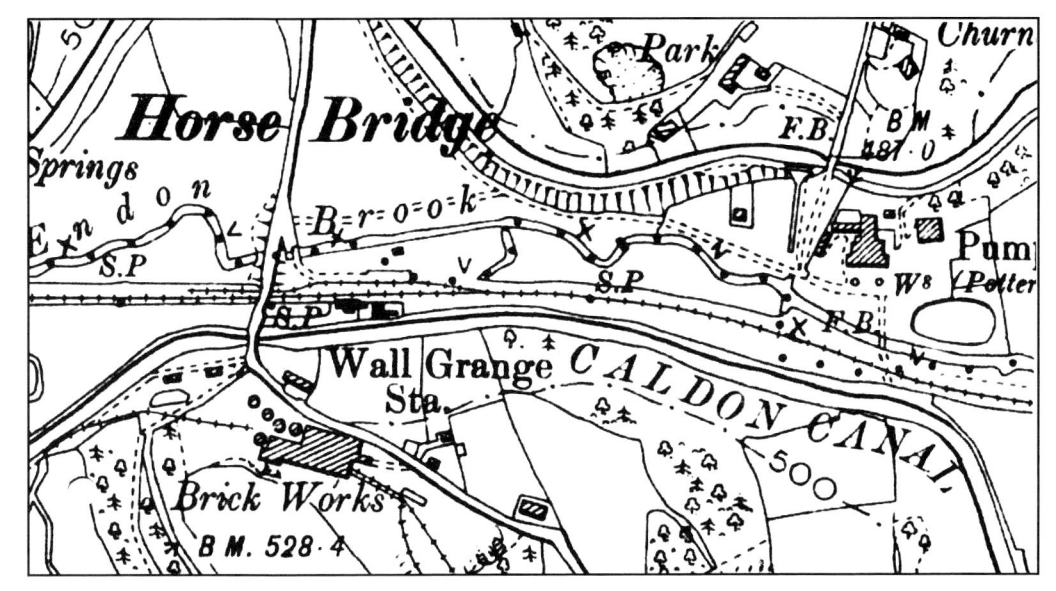

V. Wall Grange was around 1¼ miles west of Leek Brook Junction and opened in 1873 to serve a scattered rural community. The suffix was added in early LMS days for a small village half a mile to the north on the A53. The Leek Branch was built as single track but was doubled from Leek Brook to here in 1909 and on to Endon in 1910. The line follows Endon Brook, a tributary of the Churnet, gently upstream, and is flanked by two arms of the Caldon Canal, the main trunk leading to Froghall south of the railway, and the Leek Branch to its north. The map is dated 1900 and is scaled at approximately 10ins to 1 mile.

7. An eastward view from the first decade of the 20th Century sees a train departing from the single platform towards Leek. The goods siding is occupied by six wagons. The building in the left background is a water pumping station for the canals, whilst the two faint towers in the distance are at St Edward's Hospital. (Railway Station Photographs)

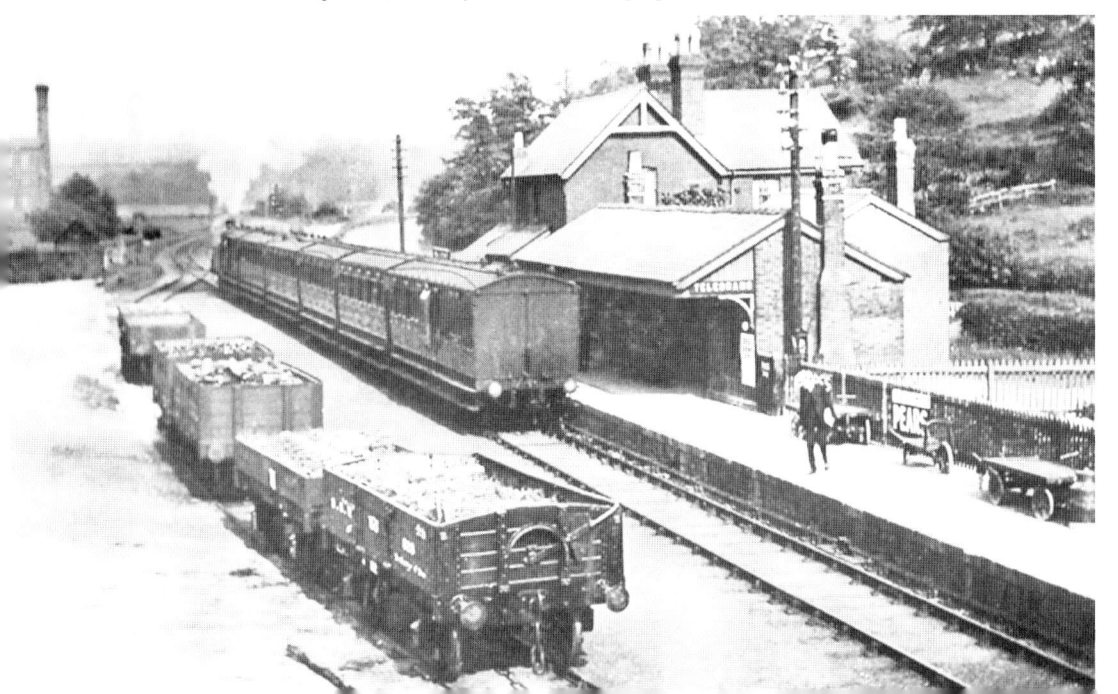

8.   A similar view taken sometime between the doubling of the line and the outbreak of war in 1914 shows a crowd of excursionists leaving a down train. The countryside round about is attractive with good walks. The new down platform is evident; the up platform has been lengthened at the east end and shortened at the west to accommodate the boarded crossing in the foreground. The siding has been slewed further north to make room for the new platform.
(Railway Station Photographs)

9.   Following withdrawal of the passenger service in 1956, the route was re-singled, retaining the down line. The down platform was removed, along with the buildings from the up platform, which itself remained intact. The station house became a private residence. Goods traffic ended from 2nd February 1989, but the line has never officially closed, being classified as 'non-operational'. There has been much tree growth, as can be seen from this view of 27th March 2018, but the track was still in situ and clear of vegetation. It was leased from Network Rail by Moorland & City Railways, an associate of Churnet Valley Rly which hopes to restore trains in the medium term at least as far as Endon. (A.C.Hartless)

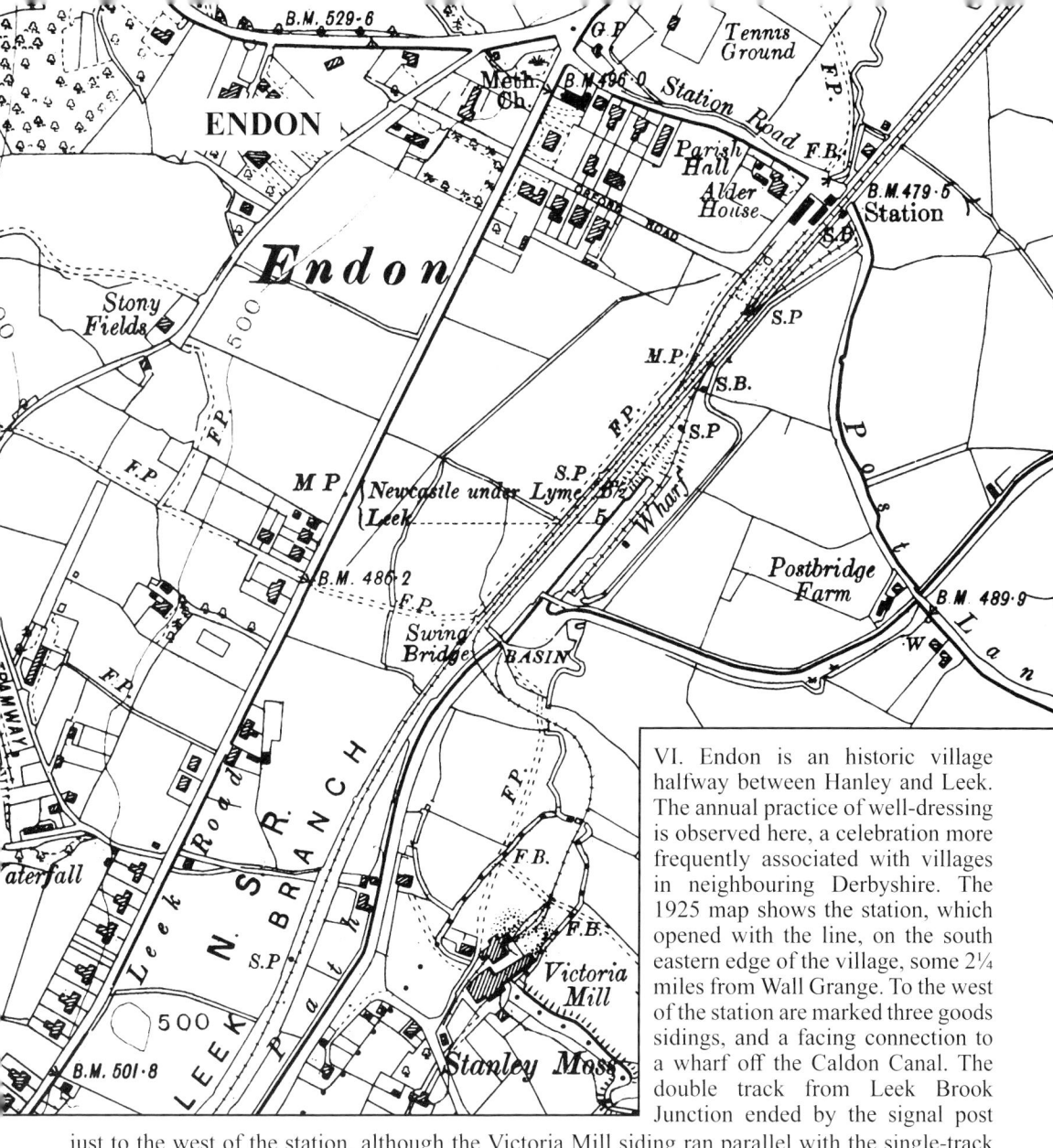

VI. Endon is an historic village halfway between Hanley and Leek. The annual practice of well-dressing is observed here, a celebration more frequently associated with villages in neighbouring Derbyshire. The 1925 map shows the station, which opened with the line, on the south eastern edge of the village, some 2¼ miles from Wall Grange. To the west of the station are marked three goods sidings, and a facing connection to a wharf off the Caldon Canal. The double track from Leek Brook Junction ended by the signal post just to the west of the station, although the Victoria Mill siding ran parallel with the single-track main line for another 30 chains or so. The Caldon Canal was opened in 1778 primarily to convey limestone quarried at Caldon Low from Froghall to customers in the Potteries and Cheshire. In 1847, it was purchased by the North Staffordshire Rly, but kept in use. By the early 20th Century it was becoming increasingly difficult to maintain, so the railway built Endon Wharf and installed a tippler for the trans-shipment of stone from rail to canal. This went into use in 1919, after which the stone traffic between Froghall and Endon transferred to rail. However, the tippler was used for only 10 years or so before declining use of the canals made trans-shipment unnecessary. Beyond the basin can be seen a siding crossing the canal by a swing bridge en route to Victoria Mill. This was established well before the coming of the railway, and its original product was flint stones. With the development of the Potteries, the mill went into the manufacture of ceramic colours and glazes. The railway connection was built in 1885 and served until 1961. The shunting locomotive from 1925 until the cessation of rail traffic was *Nina*, a lightweight battery powered unit which was the only loco allowed across the canal swing bridge.

10. The down platform was photographed from an up train; the view is undated. From left to right we can just see the 5-ton crane with a coal agent's office behind, the substantial corn store, a modest building on the platform housing the ladies' and 1st class waiting rooms, and the booking office/general waiting room at right angles to the track. The gable end of the station masters house is visible between the booking office and the down starter, to the right of which we see the level crossing. (Railway Station Photographs)

11. On Saturday 12th June 1948 class 4MT 2-6-4T LMS no. 2675 runs in with a Leek – Stoke passenger service of six coaches. The up line was added as a crossing loop sometime between 1879 and 1898, and the up platform when the route from Wall Grange was doubled in 1910. (W.A.Camwell/SLS)

12. An eastward view from 28th May 1960 shows the station to be intact down to the NSR running-in board; it was used for excursion traffic until Stoke Wakes week in August 1963. The 30 lever signal box closed in 1973 when the up line was removed. (H.B.Priestley/R.Humm coll.)

13. On 8th April 1983 nos. 25051 and 25239 accelerate a loaded sand train towards Stoke through the remains of the station. Following the closure of the signal box the level crossing was controlled by the train crews. In 2018, the platform and track were still in situ, and the platform building was the Station Kitchen, a week end café run by the Churnet Valley Railway. The booking office was demolished in the mid-1960s, but the station masters house remained as a private residence. The Endon Health Centre was built on part of the former goods yard. (I.Bailey)

STOCKTON BROOK

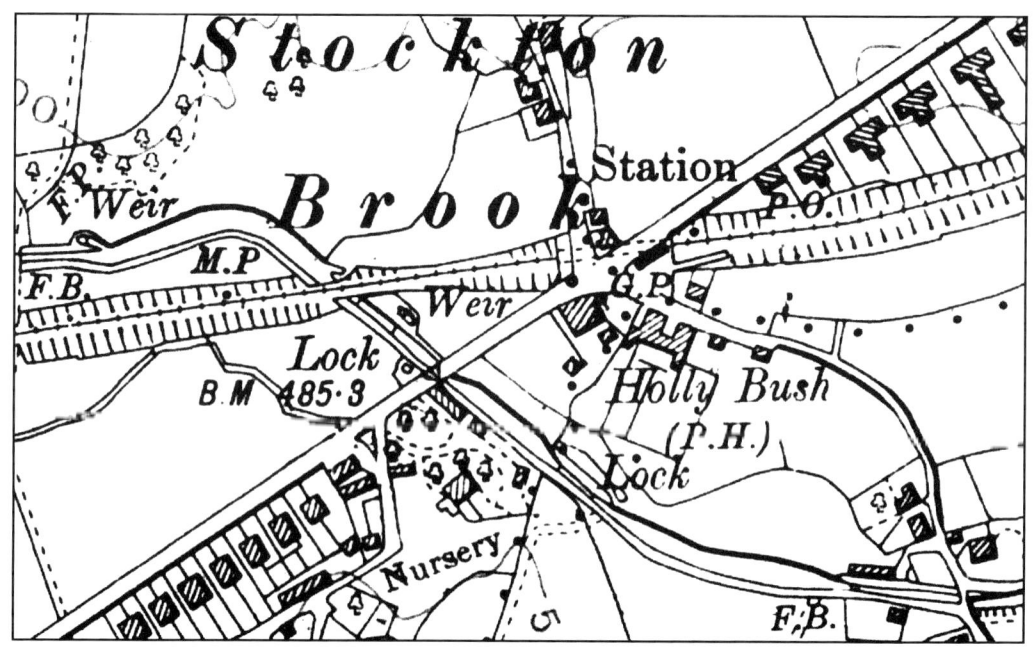

VII. Stockton Brook opened on 1st July 1896 to serve new housing along Leek Road, which crosses the line here. The station was close to the summit of the Leek Branch between Endon Brook to the east and the Head of Trent to the west, and just under one mile from Endon. There was no goods station. The proximity of the line generally to Leek Road was no bad thing in the 19th Century, but the railway was unable to compete with the proliferation of motor buses after 1900, which resulted in the closure of the uneconomic passenger service in 1956.

14. An undated view of c1935 looks eastwards from Leek Road and shows the platform to be little more than two coach lengths and provided with a small shelter. The suffix 'for Brown Edge' was added c1923. (D.Thompson/R.Humm coll.)

15. An undated westward view shows the exit ramp up to Leek Road at left, and the long skew bridge beneath the road junction. This also accommodated the single storey station building, which after closure became a shop; in 2018 it was a bathroom and kitchen showroom.
(Railway Station Photographs)

16. On a cold, wet 10th March 1984 the North West Rambler No. 3 railtour, which originated at London Euston, included Stoke to Leek Brook Junction and return in its itinerary. Nos. 25218 & 25059 were used for this leg and are seen crossing the Caldon Canal as they approach Stockton Brook en route to Leek Brook. No. 25218 was withdrawn and scrapped in the following year, but no. 25059 was acquired by the Keighley & Worth Valley Railway in 1987. (A.C.Hartless)

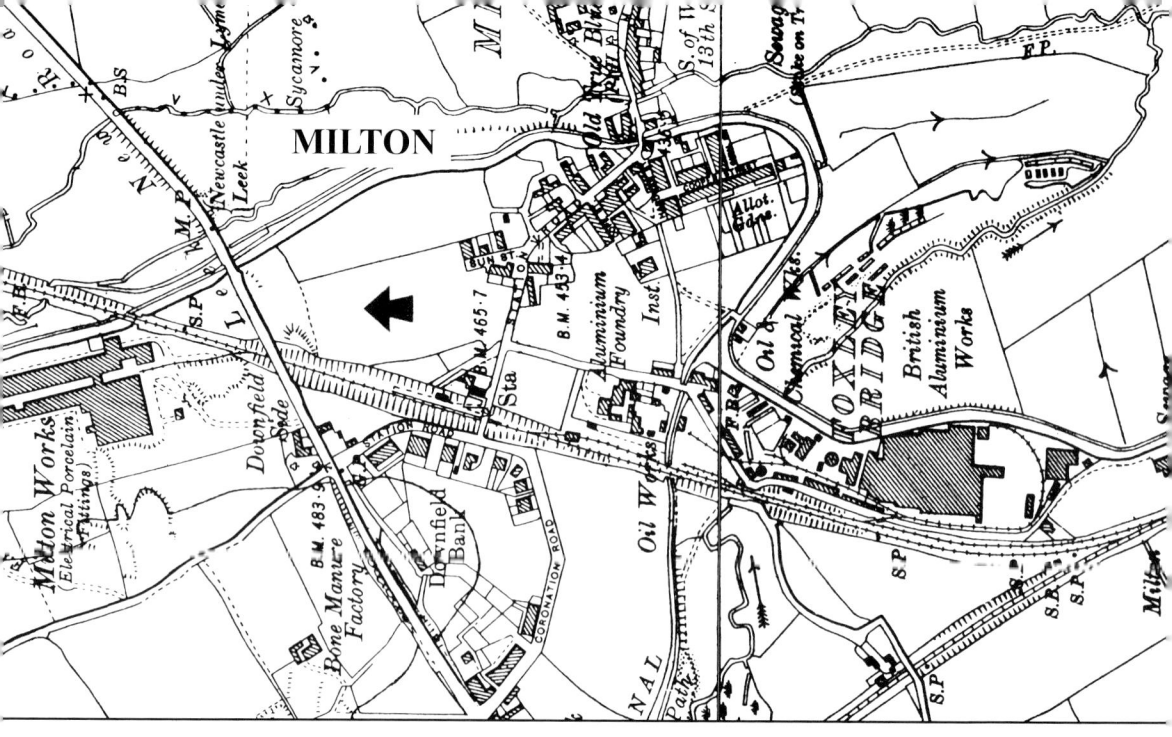

VIII. Our route runs from left to right on this map of 1922, the year in which Milton was incorporated into the county borough of Stoke-on-Trent. The station was some 1½ miles from Stockton Brook, and was situated to the west of the village. On the approach to the station the single-track line crossed the Head of Trent and then the Caldon Canal. The Milton Works of Messrs Bullers was served by both the canal and the railway and opened in 1920. South of the station was a succession of factories. The aluminium foundry of Jackson Bros. and the oil works of Cooper & Adams shared sidings which spanned the Foxley Branch canal. South of this was the oil & chemical works of Josiah Hardman, which closed in the early 1930s, and was the only factory in Milton to have its own shunting locomotive. The British Aluminium works was the first outside the USA to use the electrolytic method of manufacturing aluminium. Milton Junction marked the southern end of the Leek Branch where it trailed into the Biddulph Valley line.

17. The station opened with the line and is seen here early in the 20th century. The view is southward; beyond the platform building the exit ramp leads to street level, where the single storey booking office is prominent. Count the chimneys in the right background. (Lens of Sutton/J.Suter coll.)

18. On 13th June 1953 2-6-4T no. 42665 pauses with the 4.30pm Leek – Stoke. In 2018 the platform and track were still there, but heavily overgrown, as was most of the route from Endon to Stoke Junction. (F.W.Shuttleworth)

19. On 11th April 1986 no. 25202 is seen at Milton Junction with a Caldon Low – Witton (Birmingham) limestone train. The Biddulph Valley line formerly went off to the left, explaining the unusual angle of the signal box to the track. The box closed the following year. (P.D.Shannon)

BUCKNALL & NORTHWOOD

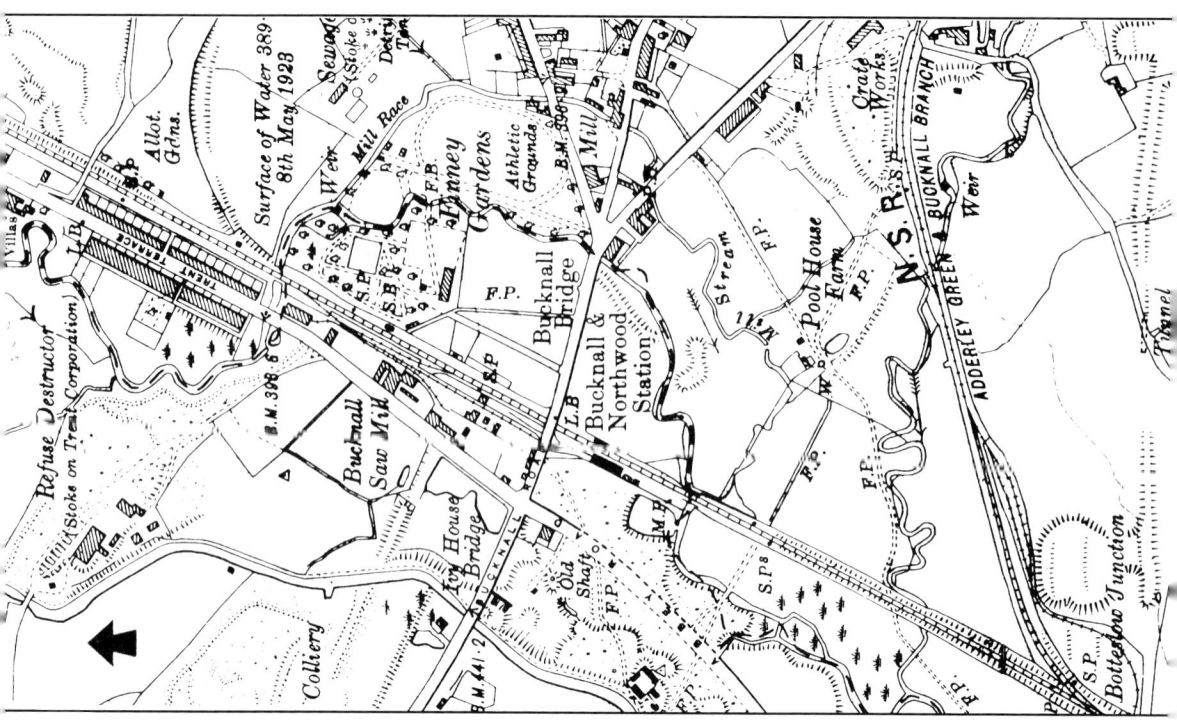

IX. Bucknall & Northwood opened with the start of the Stoke – Biddulph service on 1st June 1864 and closed for regular trains with the end of the Leek service on 5th May 1956. It was used subsequently for excursion trains, 11th August 1962 for Stoke Wakes Week being the most likely end date. The station was 2 miles south of Milton and close to the infant River Trent, which the line crosses both to north and south. The original site was north of Bucknall Road, where the station house and signalbox remained for many years afterwards, before relocating south of the bridge. This was a consequence of doubling the original single track and adding a loading bay on the up side in the area of the first station and happened before 1898.

North of the station, the 1923 revision of the map shows the course of the abandoned connection to Hanley and Bucknall Colliery going off the left upper edge; the colliery closed c1889. Similarly, the formation of the tramway from Northwood Colliery, closed c1917, is on the left lower edge; this terminated above the sidings north of the station and its coal was tipped into standard gauge wagons beneath. The sidings also served the saw mill.

South of the station was Botteslow Junction, where the Adderley Green and Bucknall Branch (AG&B) trailed in on the east side. This privately sponsored mineral line ran to Normacot on the Stoke – Derby line, a distance of around 3½ miles. It was acquired by the NSR in 1895, by which time it had been severed into two branch lines. The Bucknall branch was 2½ miles long and served the collieries at Adderley Green, which closed in 1935, and Mossfield which lasted until 1963, following which the branch closed. To the east of Botteslow Junction can be seen the course of the tramway, part of which was in tunnel, to Brookhouse Colliery which closed circa 1880. The full route of this tramway can be seen at the top of map X.

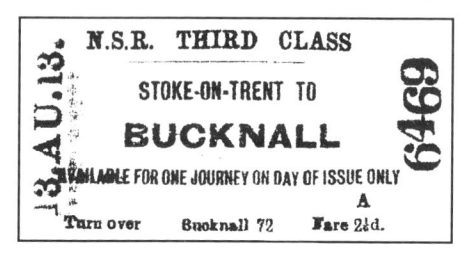

20. This southerly view from 1948 includes the AG&B line crossing the mid-ground from left to right where Botteslow Junction is visible. In centre background is Berry Hill Colliery with its two chimneys, coke ovens and conical spoil heap. The more distant heap to its right marked Fenton Colliery. Note the trailing crossover in the foreground, used by traffic leaving the goods yard behind the camera. (D.Thompson/R.Humm coll.)

21. Pathfinder Tours were able to run a special along the Leek Branch to Caldon Low on 28th May 1994, more than five years after the cessation of regular traffic. Nos. 31110 and 31185 pass the remains of the station. (M.Loader)

FENTON MANOR

X. Fenton Manor was 1¼ miles south of Bucknall & Northwood and opened on 1st October 1889 in response to urban growth. As elsewhere on the Leek-Stoke route, official closure was with effect from 7th May 1956, but the station remained available for excursion traffic until c1962. This 1900 map overlaps with sheet IX. and includes Botteslow Coal Wharf adjacent to Leek Road at the top left; this closed in 1948. The Berry Hill Coal & Iron Works was in production from 1865 to 1906, but the last pit on the associated colliery complex lasted until 1960. This was adjacent to our route and passed to the National Coal Board at the start of 1947. There was also a sizeable brick works.

22. Fenton Manor was seemingly a camera-shy station. This rare north facing view dates from 1896 and presents a most tidy appearance. The station approach is at right with the boarded crossing in the foreground giving access to the down platform. The fencing running across the background marks the course of the almost parallel Victoria Road, later the A50, linking Hanley to the left with Longton. Just visible behind the running in board at left is the portal of Fenton Manor Tunnel, which in reality was a long skew bridge beneath the road. (Science & Society Picture Library)

23. This general view of NCB Berry Hill includes coke ovens, two tall chimneys, and the headgear. Almost out of shot in the right foreground view is one of the small fleet of internal shunters, and which appears to be *Berry Hill No. 3*, a Bagnall 0-4-0ST which came here in 1947. (Apedale Heritage Centre coll.)

SOUTH OF STOKE

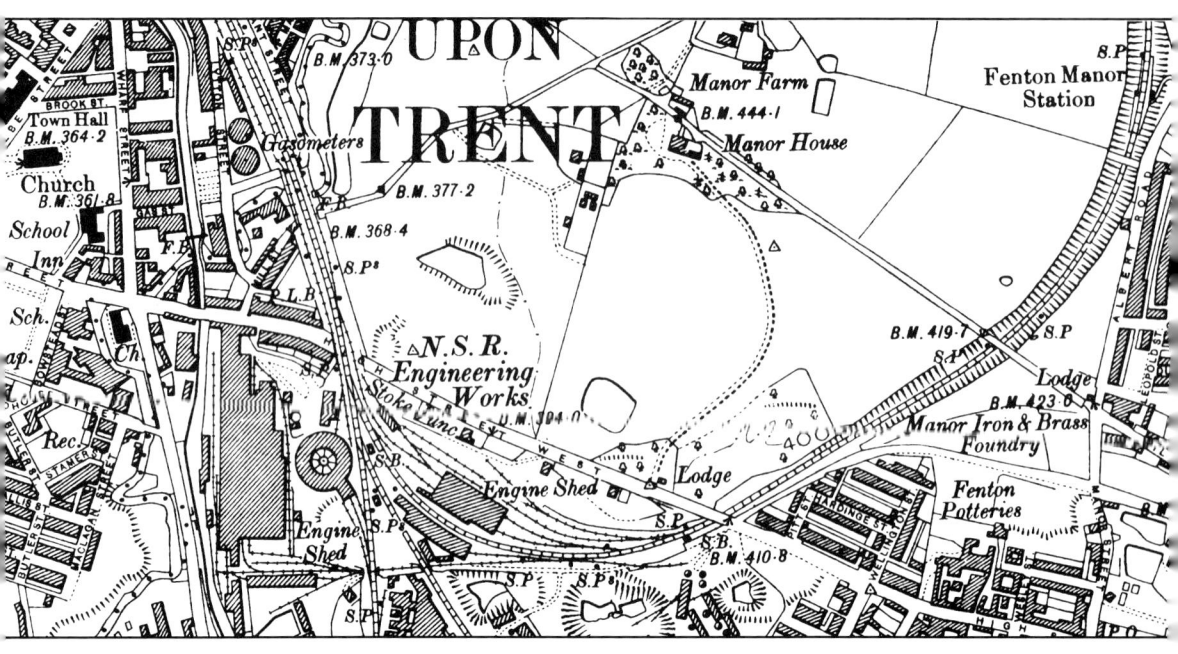

XI. South of Fenton Manor, our route turned through 180 degrees to approach Stoke-on-Trent, 1¼ miles distant, from the south. In the course of doing so, it passed Stoke loco shed, the operating centre of the NSR, before joining the combined lines from Stone and Derby at Stoke Junction, which was the end of the Biddulph Valley Line. The signal box seen in the lower centre of the map was Pratt's Sidings, which extended westwards across the line from the engine shed, and were later enlarged by the LMS, replacing the wagon repair shed which is the building between the two engine sheds on this map of 1898.

   The roundhouse was the first part of the Stoke loco shed complex to be constructed, opening around 1852 to replace smaller facilities adjacent to Stoke station. It had 23 roads, and its 50ft turntable was the only one on the site. It was used for running repairs as well as for stabling. When the need for further accommodation arose, a six road straight shed was built on the opposite side of the running lines in the early 1870s. This was later enlarged by a one road extension on the north side, and in 1905 by a two-road extension for motor trains on the south side. Improvements made by the LMS included the installation of a 150 tons capacity coaling tower. Stoke was coded 5D under the 1935 LMS loco shed reorganisation plan, which it retained until closure on 7th August 1967. Stoke Works, left of the roundhouse, opened in 1849 and was expanded in 1865 after the NSR had decided, as far as possible, to construct and maintain its own locomotives, carriages, and wagons. Altogether 192 locos were constructed here. Following the grouping of 1923, the LMS reviewed the workshops it had inherited, and the axe fell on Stoke. Loco work was transferred to Crewe and C&W to Derby, with closure completed by mid-1927, after which the premises were leased to a foundry business.

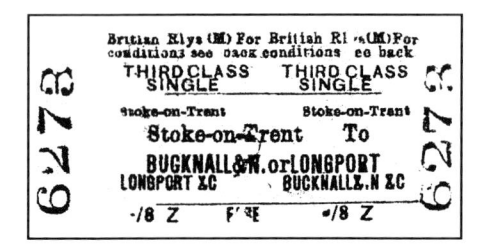

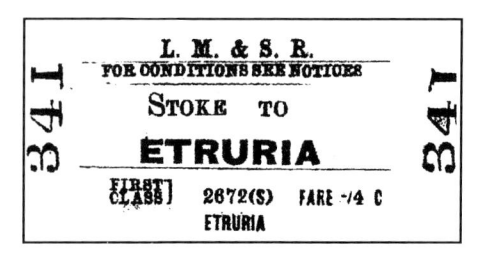

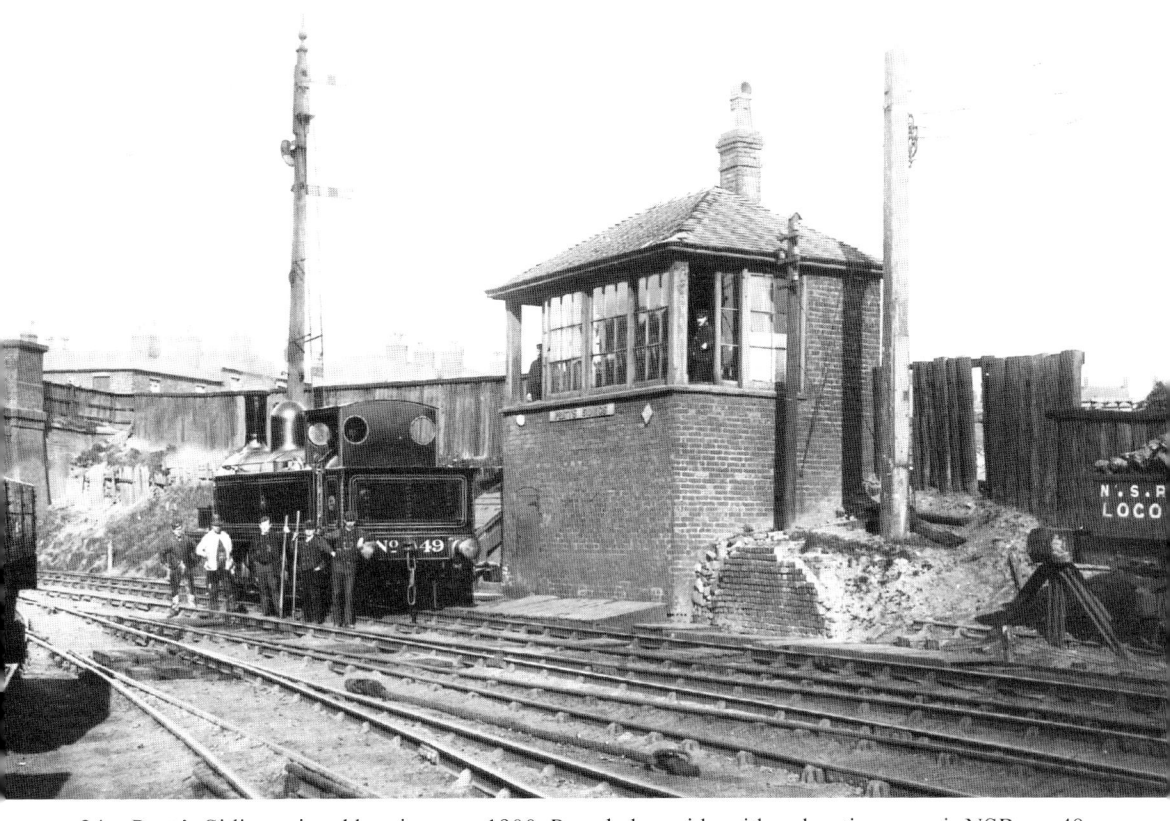

24. Pratt's Sidings signal box is seen c1900. Posed alongside with a shunting gang is NSR no. 49, a sturdy 0-6-0T built at Stoke in 1885. It lasted until 1931, latterly as LMS no. 1562. The signal box outlived it handsomely, not closing until 9th April 1972. (R.Humm coll)

25. The erecting shop at Stoke Works was photographed in 1911. There were three tracks, all fully occupied. Working conditions were very cramped, primarily because of the constrained site. (Author's coll.)

26. On Sunday 30th April 1933 the light was perfect for this view of the straight shed. Seen from Stoke Junction signalbox, the west end of the yard is full of locos coaled up for the following day's work, including former NSR D class 0-6-0T no. 1570 of 1888, which lasted until the end of 1937, beyond which is 2-6-4T no. 2346, and on the adjacent road 4F 0-6-0 no. 4308, both modern LMS locos. The nine covered shed roads can be seen; the single road extension at the left was known as The Parlour. On the right the down Biddulph Valley line curves around the two road Motor Shed. (H.C.Casserley)

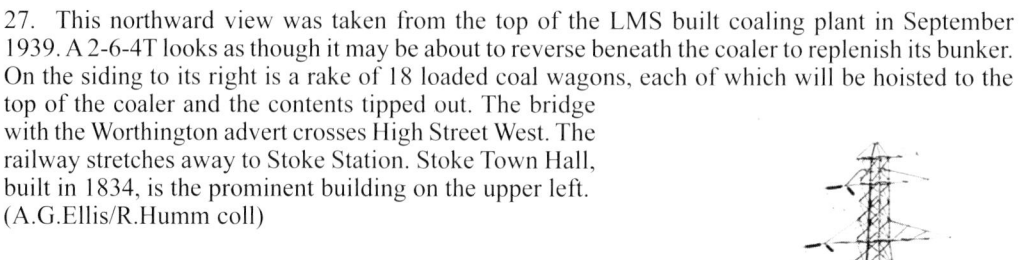

27. This northward view was taken from the top of the LMS built coaling plant in September 1939. A 2-6-4T looks as though it may be about to reverse beneath the coaler to replenish its bunker. On the siding to its right is a rake of 18 loaded coal wagons, each of which will be hoisted to the top of the coaler and the contents tipped out. The bridge with the Worthington advert crosses High Street West. The railway stretches away to Stoke Station. Stoke Town Hall, built in 1834, is the prominent building on the upper left. (A.G.Ellis/R.Humm coll)

28. This view is of the east end of the running sheds on Sunday 22nd June 1958. Half of the original building survives on the left, but the other half has been rebuilt after being for many years roofless. The locos are resident class 4 2-6-4 tanks nos. 42443 and 42590, 'Crab' 2-6-0 no. 42777 from Crewe South, and a Stanier 8F 2-8-0. (F. Hornby)

29. Stoke roundhouse was photographed on Sunday 29th March 1964 from the east side of the tracks. A BR Standard class 4 4-6-0 can be seen through the right-hand windows, its boiler reflecting the daylight within; the space above the turntable was open to air. The signal protects the junction of the Derby lines nearest the camera with the Stone lines beyond. Sadly the roundhouse did not escape the march of progress and was demolished after the shed closed. (R.S.Carpenter coll.)

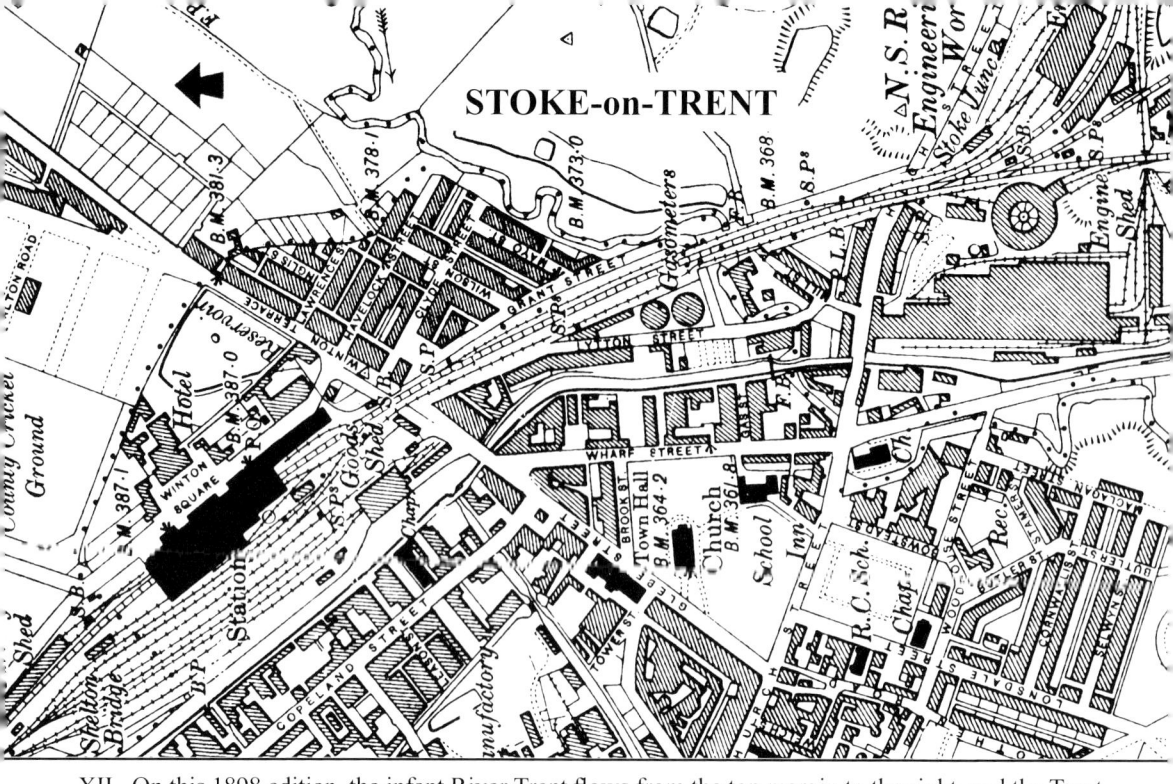

XII. On this 1898 edition, the infant River Trent flows from the top margin to the right, and the Trent & Mersey Canal from the right, west of the NSR workshops, to the lower left at Shelton Bridge. The station is preceded from the south by the bridge across Glebe Street, once the A52. The station buildings incorporated the offices of the NSR, which continued in railway usage until the 1970s. Winton Square, where the North Staffordshire Hotel faces the station, was designated a conservation area with arguably the best concentration of period buildings in the Potteries. On the west side of the station was the goods shed and yard, which included a 60ft turntable, 10ft larger than the one at Stoke loco shed. On the up side at the north end was a four-road carriage shed which was demolished around 1931. The track layout through the station is seen at its zenith, with four through roads flanked by two platforms, and the two platform Newcastle bay on the down side north end, and the extensive goods yard. In 2018, the station was fundamentally the same, but only the two through platform roads and the more easterly of the bay platform tracks remained. Everything else had been lifted.

30. This is a southward view of the station's interior c1880. There are four tracks, of which the two central roads were initially used as carriage sidings and which were open air. When the station was rebuilt in 1893-4, the arcading was replaced by an overall roof. (R.Humm coll.)

31. This is the south end of the station c1900. NSR 2-4-0 no. 19 was built at Stoke and was in traffic from 1871 until 1905. Afternoon sun reflects from its red brown livery. The driver and fireman are standing on the back of the tender, apparently moving coal forward for the next part of their journey. The starter signal is off, ready for the train to depart. The buildings behind were subsequently enlarged, but the signal remained until the end of mechanical signalling in 1966, albeit with upper quadrants fitted by the LMS. (G.T.Boulton/J.Suter coll.)

32. At the north end of the station, LMS 0-6-2T no. 2248 runs along the down through road on 6th July 1931 with a local trip working, possibly bound for Shelton Steel Works. This loco was built at Stoke in 1908 as NSR no. 156 of class 'New L' and lasted until 1937. Glebe Street signal box can be seen beyond the station, behind the train's brake van. (LGRP/R.Humm coll.)

33. Glebe Street signal box is seen around 1960. This dated from 1880 and had 65 levers. Alterations to the brickwork are apparent where windows have been inserted or enlarged to allow natural light to the locking room. The box closed in 1966 with the advent of colour light signalling controlled by the new Stoke Power Signal Box (PSB). (R.Humm coll.)

34. Stoke North signal box, pictured in September 1964 from a passing train, was an LMS design of 1931 with 120 levers. It stood on the down side of the tracks 200 yards north of the station, opposite the site of the NSR box it replaced. Stoke goods yard is behind and beyond it; there were 14 sidings following enlargement by the LMS in the early 1930s. The box was another 1966 closure. (R.J.Essery/R.Carpenter coll.)

➔ 35. Lytton Street, just south of the station, has been witness to countless trains. Sometime in 1964 a grimy 8F 2-8-0 awaits the signal from Glebe Street box to draw its train into Stoke Goods Yard. Note the 5D coaler in the background. The goods lines were removed during the 1990s and ultimately the yard was given over to car parking.
(C.T.Gifford/Science & Society Picture Library)

⬇ 36. A northward view on 10th June 1977 sees class 304 EMU no. 019 running into platform 1 with the 16.45 Manchester Piccadilly - Stafford. No. 86034 has the green light from signal SE84 to leave platform 2 with the 14.55 Euston – Manchester. In the left background a coated gentleman, close to the site of Stoke North signal box, is supervising a shunt in Stoke Yard. The angular building to the rear of the EMU is Stoke PSB, which went into operation on 17th July 1966. The track in the left foreground, controlled by signal SE85 is the bay platform 3. (T.Heavyside)

37. A southward view inside Stoke station from 2nd June 1984 has the 14.20 Crewe – Cleethorpes departing from platform 1, formed by a class 108 DMU. The high roof line admits plenty of natural light which shows the architectural details to good effect. Note especially the archway leading outside to Winton Square. (B.Morrison)

38. The station's frontage, seen here on a spring morning in 1987, speaks eloquently of the confidence in the railway age of the 1840s. Designed by Sir Henry Hunt, the station opened in 1848 along with much of the NSR's network. The NSR was headquartered here; its Boardroom was behind the impressive bay window on the upper floor, above which the company's crest can still be seen. The building's style has been described as 'robust Jacobean manor house'. Its red brick and dressed stone have been sensitively restored after decades of industrial pollution. (I.Bailey)

NORTH of STOKE - COCKSHUTE

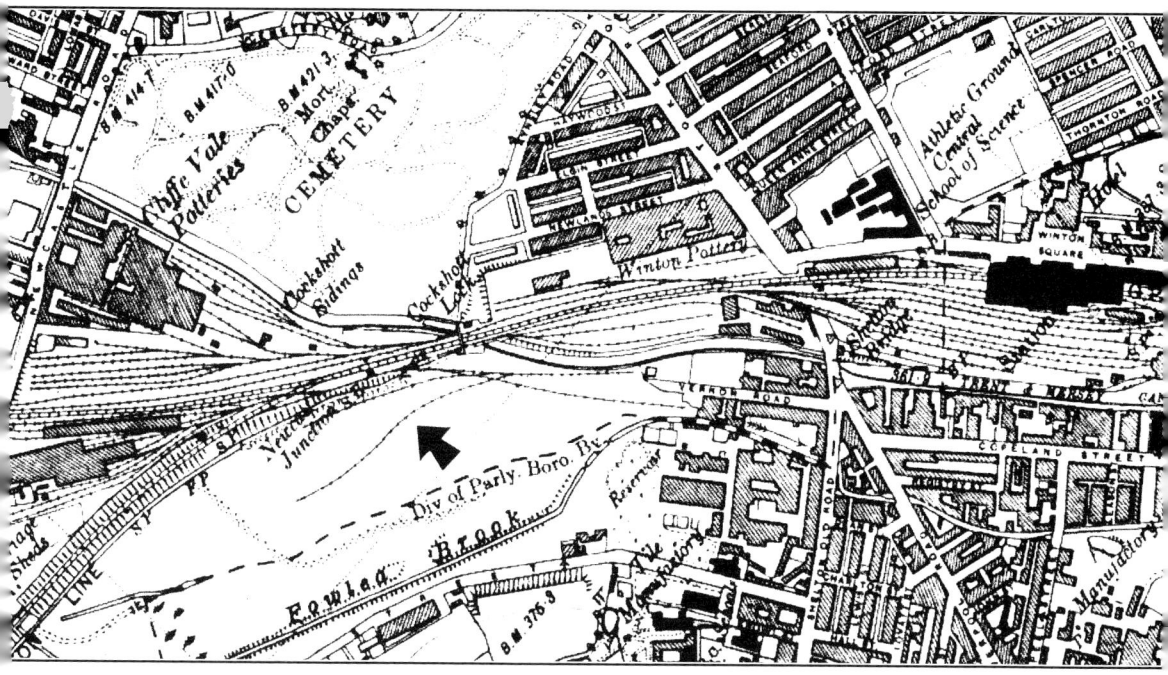

XIII. Our route continues from right to left. Leaving Stoke, the line crosses Stoke Road, which links Stoke and Hanley. The sidings on the up side close to Winton Pottery were the LNWR's Stoke Goods depot. On the opposite side of the main line was Shelton Wharf, where merchandise was exchanged between canal, rail and road. This was followed by the bridge across the Trent & Mersey Canal, which was opened in 1777 and acquired by the NSR in 1847. Beyond the canal bridge a backshunt gave access to sidings between the canal and Fowlea Brook; these were later the site of the Cliffe Vale china clay terminal (see picture 69 in *Branch Lines around Market Drayton*). At Newcastle Junction the line to Newcastle-under-Lyme of 1852 branched off to the west; this closed from 8th March 1966. Opposite can be seen Cockshott Sidings, known in later years as Cockshute. This yard was enlarged in the mid-1930s and was last used in the mid-1980s. Back on the down side are shown the main carriage sheds of the NSR, by which they were known as Cliffe Vale. British Railways built a three road diesel depot on the site of the larger shed. This was in use from 1957 to 1966 servicing DMUs and shunters but was surplus to requirements after the closure of the Loop Line and the electrification of Stafford to Manchester local trains. The smaller of the NSR sheds remained in use for stabling of diesel locos and units until the late 1980s. Newcastle Road, leading to Hanley, originally crossed the line by a level crossing which was replaced in the early 1870s by a five-span bridge.

> **Further pictures of Stoke-on-Trent can be seen in the following albums:** *Derby to Stoke-on-Trent*, *Branch Lines around Market Drayton* **and** *Rugeley to Stoke-on-Trent*.

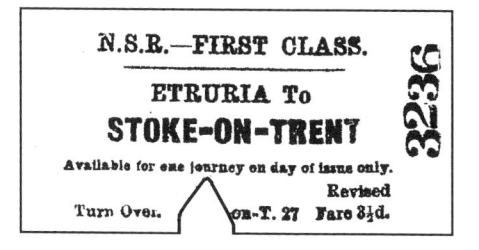

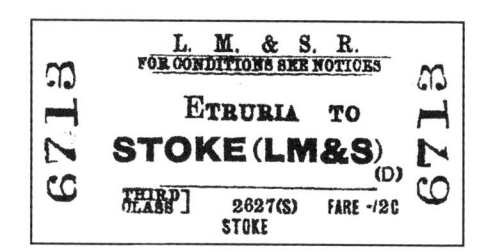

39. On 15th March 1962 'Crab' 2-6-0 no. 42894 runs tender first from Stoke towards the Newcastle branch with empty coal wagons. The branch goes off the left margin, in front of Cockshute carriage shed, which is at a lower level and partially obscured by a three-bracket signal and a telegraph pole. A 2-6-4T is standing at the top of the rise from the shed with a rake of stock. Newcastle Junction signal box was an NSR structure which closed in 1966. To its right is a 350hp diesel shunter with an up transfer freight. Between this and no. 42894 is part of Cockshute Sidings, whose signal box can be seen above the 'Crab's' cab. Etruria Gasworks dominates the background. (F.W.Shuttleworth)

40. The BR diesel depot at Cockshute is seen on Sunday 6th May 1962. LMS carriage stock is parked on the left. The shed is empty, but the yard contains a couple of 350hp diesel shunters and some Birmingham Railway Carriage & Wagon Co (BRCW) DMUs. After its early closure the shed was let as a factory. (R.S.Carpenter)

41. A view from June 1979 features no. 40125 as well as examples of classes 08, 25 and 47, all typical of the period. We are looking from west to east, across the yard of the former BR diesel depot to the NSR carriage shed, beyond which runs the main line. (Rail-Online)

42. On the evening of 29th April 1983 we look north from the opposite side of the tracks. OLE structures compromise the view across the running lines, but Cockshute carriage shed can be seen in the left background; an electric locomotive is stabled alongside it. No. 08470 is shunting Cockshute Yard, most of which is empty. Newcastle Road bridge can be seen above the shunter and its wagons, also Cockshute Sidings signal box, an LMS structure from the mid-1930s which closed soon after this picture was taken. Twyfords Sanitaryware and Etruria Gasworks fill the background. A solitary barge is tied up on the Trent & Mersey Canal above Cockshutt Lock in a winding hole that reflects the industrial surroundings. (A.C.Hartless)

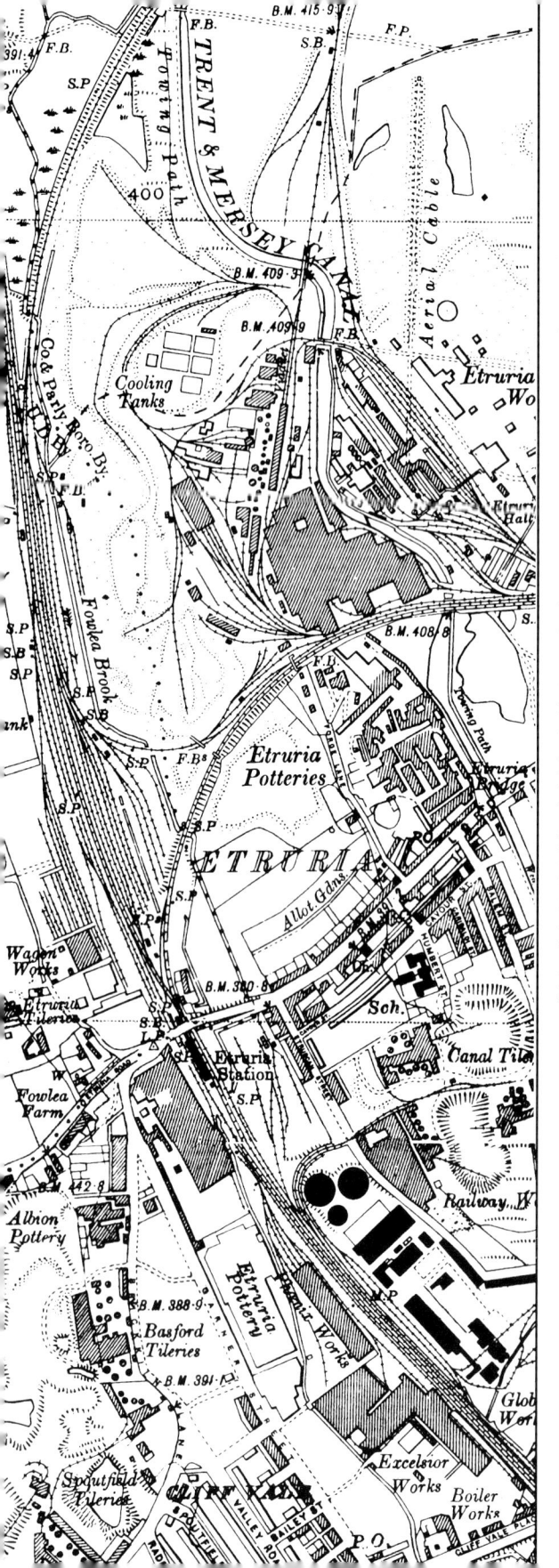

ETRURIA

XIV. Josiah Wedgwood relocated his expanding pottery business from Burslem to a greenfield site in 1769, and called it Etruria, after the pre-Roman kingdom in central Italy which was lastingly famous for its ceramics. The railway follows the course of Fowlea Brook northwards. The black structures to the east of the railway, near the foot of this 1947 map, were the Etruria gasworks, one of the largest in the UK, which supplied coal gas across the Potteries from 1904 until 1971. Etruria station was originally sited north of Etruria Road, but was relocated from 1st May 1878 as shown, some 1¼ miles from Stoke. The train service was steadily reduced, ultimately to two northbound early morning Stoke – Manchester trains, and ceased after 30th September 2005, a rare closure in the first decade of the 21st century. The station was demolished and the tracks realigned to increase the maximum line speed. North of the station the Hanley Branch, to which we shall return, diverged eastward, after which came Grange Sidings. These were latterly the main exchange sidings with Shelton Steelworks. North of these the freight only Grange Branch went off north eastward to Grange Wharf at Burslem. This was opened in 1872 by the NSR, and after the closure of Grange Wharf in 1950 the truncated line became part of Shelton Steelworks. A development after the publication of this map was the upgrading of Wolstanton Colliery, connected to the main line on the west side close to the top of the map. This was in production from 1963 to 1985.

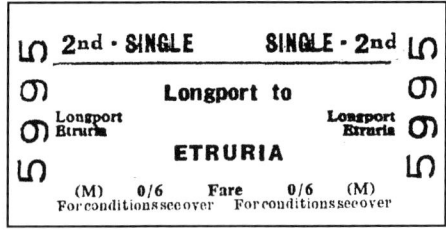

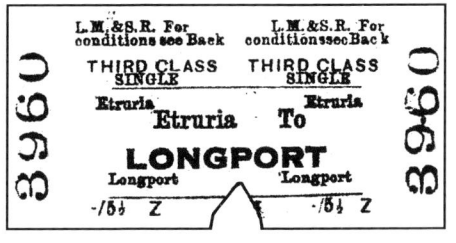

43. On 9th July 1932 an unidentified 'Prince of Wales' class 4-6-0 comes under Etruria Road with what looks like a secondary passenger service down the main line. Above the loco can be seen the street level booking office, and beyond that the gasworks, whilst Etruria Junction signal box, another 1966 closure, is visible above the tender. (E.R.Morten/J.Suter coll.)

44. Looking in the opposite direction on the same day, 'Claughton' class 4-6-0 no. 5975 *Talisman* approaches Etruria Junction under clear signals with the up 'Lancastrian'. This ran from Manchester London Road and collected through carriages from various towns in East Lancashire at Stockport, before running non-stop from Stoke to London Euston. The extensive slag heap of Shelton Steelworks forms the backdrop, partially screened by a huge Union Jack bearing the legend 'Shelton'. (E.R.Morten/J.Suter coll.)

45. On 31st July 1937 a 4F 0-6-0 comes off the Hanley branch at Etruria Junction with a mixed freight. The building behind the loco marks the site of the original station. Beyond is the Etruria part of Shelton Bar with its extensive slag heap on the left. (R.Humm coll.)

46. 29th July 1963 was evidently a lovely summer's day. Class 8F 2-8-0 no. 48120 is running slowly backwards along the down goods line whilst a track gang is fettling the siding on the up side. Etruria was an island platform station; the passenger lines were flanked by the goods lines. The substantial booking office fronting Etruria Road is seen far right. The exit to the street was by staircase from the far end of the platform. To the left we see the factory of Wengers Ltd, makers of colours, chemicals, glazes etc for the pottery, tile & brick industries. Wolstanton village is atop the distant hill, its church spire just visible, with the twin towers of Wolstanton Colliery in the far-right background. Another steam loco can be seen in Grange Sidings through the right-hand arch. (H.B.Priestley/R.Humm coll.)

47. On 17th June 1993, no. 56069 *Thornaby TMD* is seen shunting a heavy train of loaded bogie steel carriers onto the Grange Branch prior for departure to Tees Dock. On the left is Grange Junction signal box which was in use between 1966 and 2002; it had 75 levers and replaced a much older NSR box. The buildings in the background comprise the Shelton Steelworks rolling mill, opened in 1964. This was the final major investment on the site and closed in 2000, marking the end of heavy industry, and heavy haul railfreight, in North Staffordshire. (P.D.Shannon)

48. On 27th March 1999, DMU no. 156401 is seen passing with the 15.31 Manchester Airport – Skegness on the up passenger line, running away from the camera. At this date there were four platform structures, from left to right: the old lamp room, a flat roofed open fronted shelter, a flat roofed store (boarded up), and the old platform building of LMS design, now shorn of its hipped roof and canopies; locked out of use. The tall building above the leading coach is Twyfords Sanitaryware. On the skyline is Holy Trinity Church, Hartshill, designed by Gilbert Scott. (A.C.Hartless)

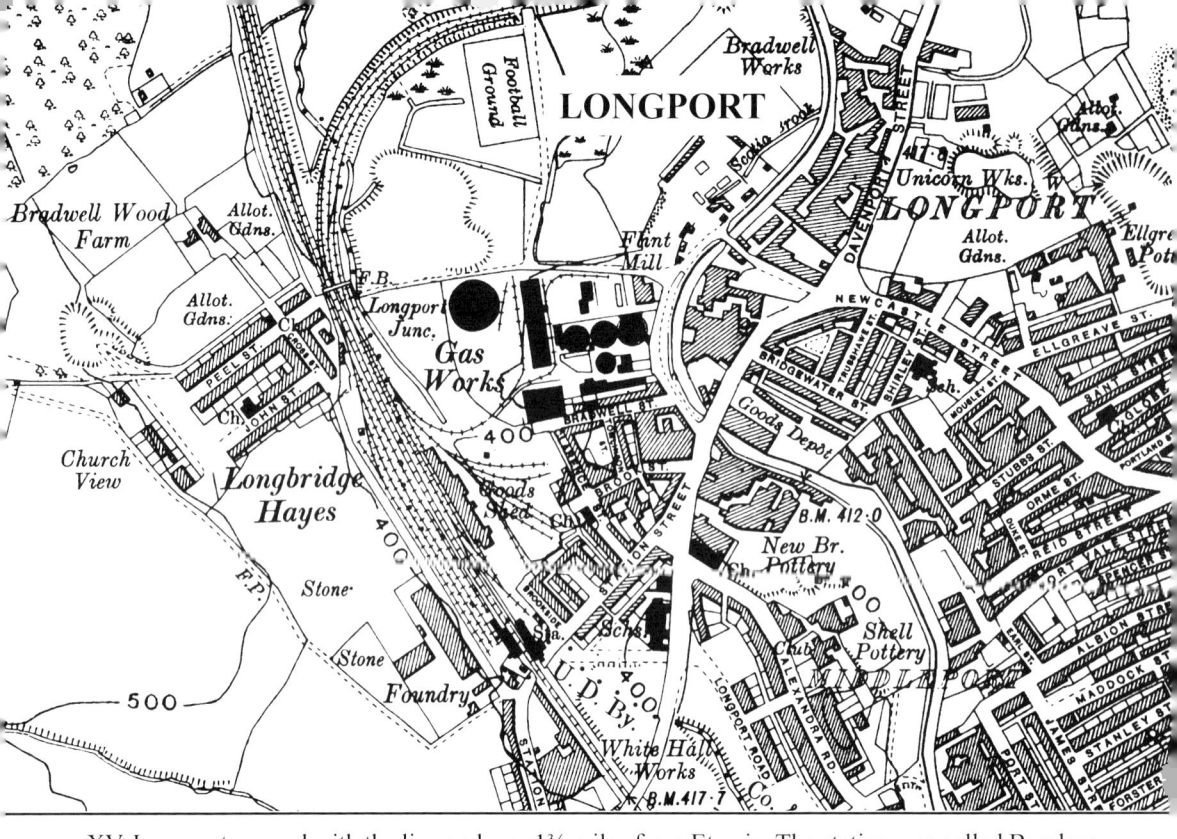

XV. Longport opened with the line and was 1¾ miles from Etruria. The station was called Burslem until 1873 when another of that name (pictures 90 – 92) opened on the Potteries Loop Line one mile to the east. At Longport Junction the goods only Tunstall (or Pinnox) Branch of 1875 diverged north eastward, connecting with the Potteries Loop Line (map XXVIII); this closed in 1964.

49. The photographer has his back to the signal box in obtaining this northward view from c1950, illustrating the level crossing and the original buildings, to which canopies of different styles have been added. Note on the end of the up side building decorative dark blue patterns in the otherwise red brickwork, a common feature on the NSR. (Railway Station Photographs)

50. North Staffs local passenger services were dieselised from 3rd March 1958, mostly by 3-car BRCW multiple units, later class 104. On 28th May 1960 the 2.20pm Crewe – Derby arrives, led by power car M50474. Note Longton Junction signal box in the left background, whilst the goods station is at right, with the gasworks behind. Shunting the goods yard is 4F 0-6-0 no. 44536. (H.B.Priestley/R.Humm coll.)

51. This post-electrification view from 1st September 1970 shows that Longport signal box, dating from 1880, was retained to operate the level crossing. The structure taking shape across the tracks is a new footbridge which allowed both crossing and box to be abolished in 1972. (H.B.Priestley/R.Humm coll.)

52. After the demise of the Speedlink network in July 1991, BR continued to carry wagonload freight between mainland Europe and around 40 destinations in the UK. One of those trains ran from Bescot to Crewe Basford Hall, calling at Stafford, Grange Sidings and Longport. No. 47312 arrives at Longport with a runner wagon and vans of various types on 5th August 1991. The terminal at Longport, the former goods station seen on the left, remained in railway ownership until the late 1990s. It was later converted into a locomotive maintenance facility for Electro-Motive Diesel (EMD). The down sidings on the right were used to store wagons, including those on their way to the Marcroft wagon repair depot south of Stoke. Longport Junction signal box was an LMS box which was in use from 1939 to 2002 and had originally 70 levers. (P.D.Shannon)

53. This final view north dates from 18th July 2012 as a Pendolino runs past with the 12.15 Manchester Piccadilly – London Euston. The up side building was listed Grade II in 1972, and is well cared for, at least externally. A small unobtrusive shelter catered for the modern traveller on each platform. (A.C.Hartless)

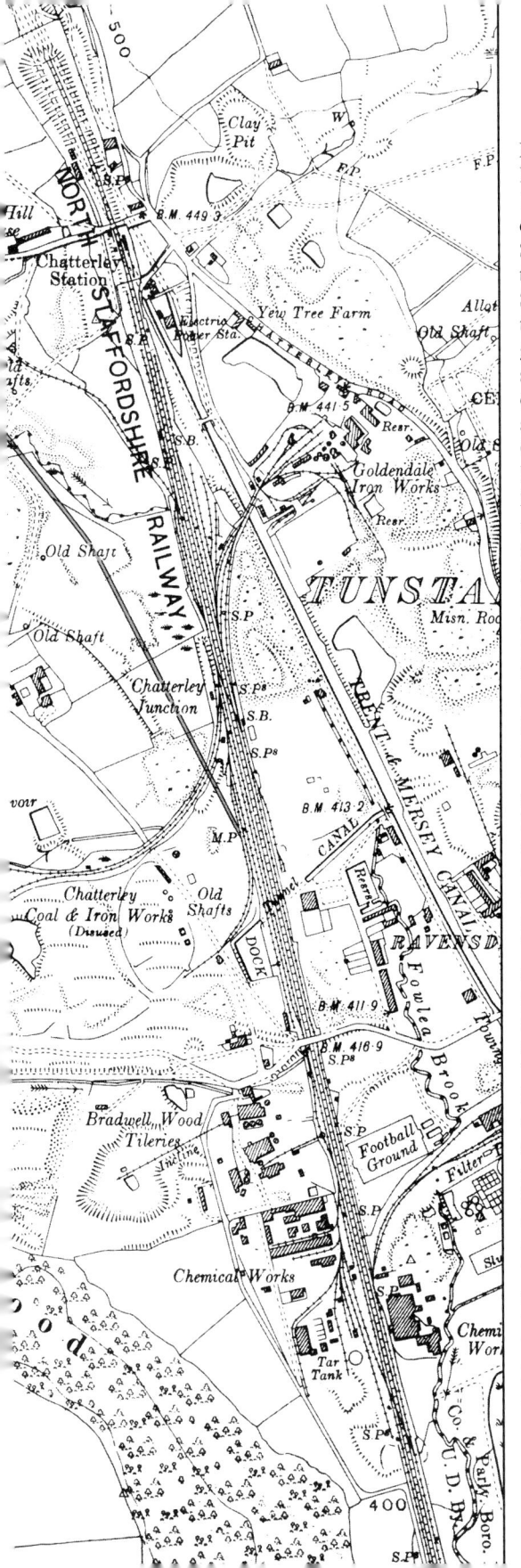

CHATTERLEY

XVI. Chatterley was 1½ miles north of Longport. It opened in January 1864 and was called Tunstall until 1873 when a station of that name (pictures 93 to 95) opened on the Potteries Loop Line one mile to the east. Services at Chatterley diminished in consequence, and the station eventually closed with effect from 27th September 1948. The site was abandoned entirely when the Harecastle Deviation opened. Chatterley had no goods station, but the line between there and Longport served numerous industries. Near the foot of the map, chemical works are shown on both sides of the line at Bradwell Wood, both the property of Staffordshire Chemicals. These operated from the 1880s until 1965. Bradwell Sidings signal box served from 1889 until 2002. The line going east below the football ground served a colliery and tileries. On the left is shown the site of Chatterley Coal & Iron Works, which closed as long ago as 1901. The goods only line running west from Chatterley Junction can be seen branching into two. The southward line ran to collieries at Chesterton (closed 1922) and Parkhouse (closed 1968), whilst the other linked to the NSR's Audley Branch, serving collieries at Talke Pits (closed 1928) and Bignall End (closed 1947). Goldendale Ironworks to the east of the line was in production from 1841 to 1971.

From Stoke, the line has followed the Fowlea Brook upstream to what is known as the Chatterley Valley. North of Chatterley station the shortest onward route was through a ridge of higher ground forming the watershed between the Trent and Dane basins, a route which followed closely the Trent & Mersey Canal and where both canal and railway required tunnels. The first canal tunnel was completed in 1777 and was over 1½ miles long. This was abandoned in 1914. A parallel but larger second tunnel was opened in 1827 and in 2018 was still in use. The rail route was very similar to the canal's, but at a slightly higher level. There were three tunnels: from south to north their lengths were 1,750 yds, 180 yds and 130 yds with short cuttings between. When electrification of the route was approved the tunnels presented a problem: there was insufficient clearance to install overhead wires, and South Tunnel in particular was suffering from mining subsidence. The chosen solution was to abandon the original alignment and build a new railway around the obstruction to the west. This left the original route south of Chatterley Junction and has been marked on the map. South Tunnel was abandoned, and Middle Tunnel was replaced by a new Harecastle Tunnel 310 yds long, immediately north of which the deviation re-joined the old alignment. North Tunnel was opened out. The deviation came into use from 27th June 1966. It was a little over two miles long, being 15 chains longer than the original line. The ruling gradient was 1 in 80 compared with 1 in 330 on the old route.

54. Pictures of Chatterley station are rare. This post closure view dates from May 1950, looking northwards to the southern portal of Harecastle South Tunnel. The line is climbing at 1 in 330. The station is derelict; coping stones, lighting and signage have been removed.
(D.Thompson/R.Humm coll.)

55. This is a northward view from 12th April 1962 taken south of Chatterley Junction, whose signal box (1896 – 1966) can be seen above the rear of the train. The loco is 4F 0-6-0 no. 44299 of Alsager shed hauling empty coal wagons. The four rightmost tracks are running lines. The building behind the loco was the one-time Port Vale Inn, which gave its name to Port Vale Football Club, which played its first few seasons nearby in the early 1880s before relocating to Burslem. Behind that can be seen Goldendale Ironworks. In 2018 this view had changed almost out of recognition. The Harecastle Deviation begins roughly where the middle of the train is passing, and the A527 Reginald Mitchell Way bridges the two remaining tracks. (F.W.Shuttleworth)

56. Aerial photography was used in the construction of the deviation, and this northward view from early 1966 shows it nearing completion. The Chesterton Branch was bisected by the new line and was realigned to make a facing connection with the main line south of the deviation. The Port Vale Inn at the lower right provides a link with the previous picture. (BRB)

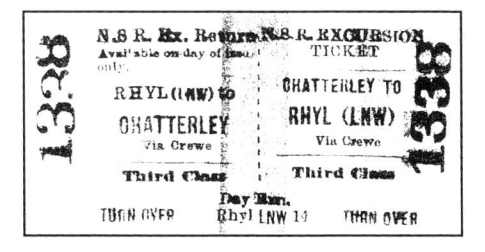

57. On 29th August 1967 no. D4109 brings a load of coal down from Parkhouse Colliery towards Bradwell Sidings along the Chesterton Branch. Parkhouse, one mile south-west of Chatterley Junction, was the last deep colliery hereabout and had less than a year left. The loco was one of only 26 of the 1,193 350hp diesel shunters built by BR between 1952 and 1962 with a higher top speed of 27mph. Under TOPS the standard design became class 08 and the faster ones class 09; D4109 became no. 09021 in 1974. (M.G.Fell)

58. No. 58019 *Shirebrook Colliery* is seen at Chatterley Valley disposal point on 19th June 1993. This opened in August 1988 as a loading point for opencast coal brought in by road, and which closed soon after the date of this visit. The train is setting back to access the main line, which can be seen behind it, prior to departure to Ironbridge power station. We are looking south east towards Burslem, close to the south end of the Harecastle deviation. (P.D.Shannon)

KIDSGROVE

XVII. Our original route comes in at the bottom right margin where it is in Harecastle South Tunnel. Close inspection indicates the railway tunnel was built above and between the two canal tunnels. The line is in a cutting close to Nelson Pit before passing through Harecastle Middle Tunnel, then in a second cutting before passing through Harecastle North Tunnel. On leaving this the line crosses the canal before reaching Harecastle Junction which precedes Harecastle Station. This has four platforms, two on the main line to Macclesfield and two on the Crewe branch which goes off the left of the map. The mineral railway marked to the east of the line ran to the slag reduction plant of Tarmac which is shown close to the reservoirs at the foot of the map. The Harecastle deviation of 1966 has been superimposed, see map XVI above.

The station has had several changes of name. It opened with the two lines on 9th October 1848 when it was called Harecastle & Kidsgrove. In the 1850s it was known at different times as Harecastle Junction, Kidsgrove Junction, and Kidsgrove Junction (Harecastle). From 15th November 1875 it was renamed Harecastle when Kidsgrove Station (pictures 103 & 104) opened nearby on the Potteries Loop Line. On 2nd October 1944 it became Kidsgrove Central, and the suffix was dropped from 18th April 1966. The goods station can be seen on the up side of the main line north of the station, and there were also two sidings on the down side of the Crewe branch.

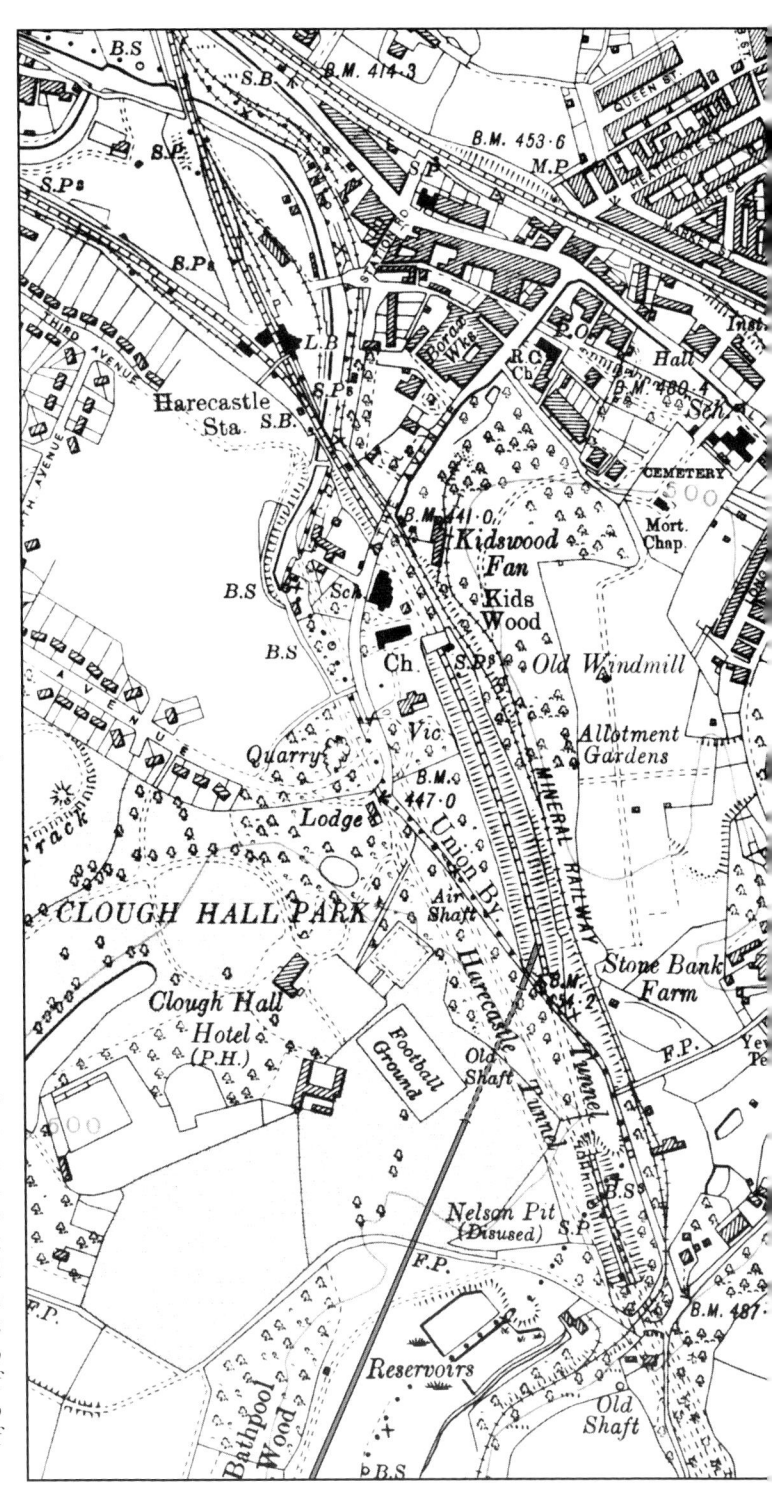

59. A postcard view from the first decade of the 20th century includes E class 0-6-0 no. 75 posed at the up Macclesfield platform. Left is Harecastle Junction (latterly Kidsgrove Central Junction) signal box which served from 1904 to 1965 and which had 31 levers. The Crewe Branch curves westward with its separate platforms. A lengthy footbridge links the four platforms with the modest ticket office etc on the right. A glimpse of the goods station can be had far right, above the two coal wagons. The Trent & Mersey Canal towpath forms the foreground. The track layout was little different in 2018. (R.Humm coll.)

60. This view from the same era is eastward across the station. The Crewe lines are in the foreground with a down coal train passing. The Macclesfield lines are beyond. Note the running in board 'Harecastle, change for Alsager, Crewe, the Loop, Audley and Sandbach lines'. Behind that is a coal merchant's office in the goods yard. The town of Kidsgrove fills much of the background, whilst the smoking chimney in the right distance marks Birchenwood Colliery. The advertisements liberally dotted around the station are worth closer inspection; several of the offerings could still be enjoyed in 2018. (Railway Station Photographs)

61. We see the exterior of what was then Kidsgrove Central on 5th August 1952. The lightweight buildings are a contrast with general NSR practice, although the entrance expresses a restrained grandeur. The signal box is visible on the left. The stop block at the right indicates the extremity of the goods yard, reduced in the years since picture 59. (LGRP/R.Humm coll.)

Bradshaw Guide, 1866.

Kidsgrove to Crewe.

This is a short line from Kidsgrove to Crewe, about 9 miles, for the convenience of the salt district of Cheshire, communicating with the line from Crewe to Burton, and so on to the eastern coast. It also opens out a valuable connection with Liverpool and the midland districts. Leaving this ancient seat of the earthenware manufacture—a district now also vieing with the southern part of the county in certain branches of the iron trade—the train enters the Harecastle tunnel, by Telford (1¾ mile), passing through a hill previously perforated by two tunnels of the Trent and Mersey canal.

62. On 27th April 1963, class 4F 0-6-0 no. 44548 stands at the up Crewe platform with the RCTS 'Cheshire Rambler' rail tour. The train has arrived from Crewe before setting off in the opposite direction for a run along the Sandbach Branch, hence it is 'wrong line'. Note the trackless down bay on the right which was used for the sparse passenger services on the lines to Wheelock and Keele, which were withdrawn in 1930 and 1931 respectively. (J.Faithfull/RCTS)

63. As part of the electrification scheme, a new signal box with 50 levers was built on the opposite side of the tracks and was in use from 1965 to 2002. On 10th June 1977, no. 47125 takes the Crewe line with empty fuel tanks from Longport to Stanlow. The ironwork of the station footbridge survived modernisation. (T.Heavyside)

64. On 18th July 2012, EMU no. 323227 departs with the Northern Rail 13.58 Stoke – Manchester Piccadilly. The brick building on platform 2 is V shaped and also serves the up Crewe platform; it has been shorn of its canopies and chimneys since picture 60. In NSR days there was a down bay platform left of where the train is situated. The main station buildings at right date from 1965. In late 2018 Network Rail announced a plan to install lifts and a replacement footbridge to give step-free access to all four platforms. (A.C.Hartless)

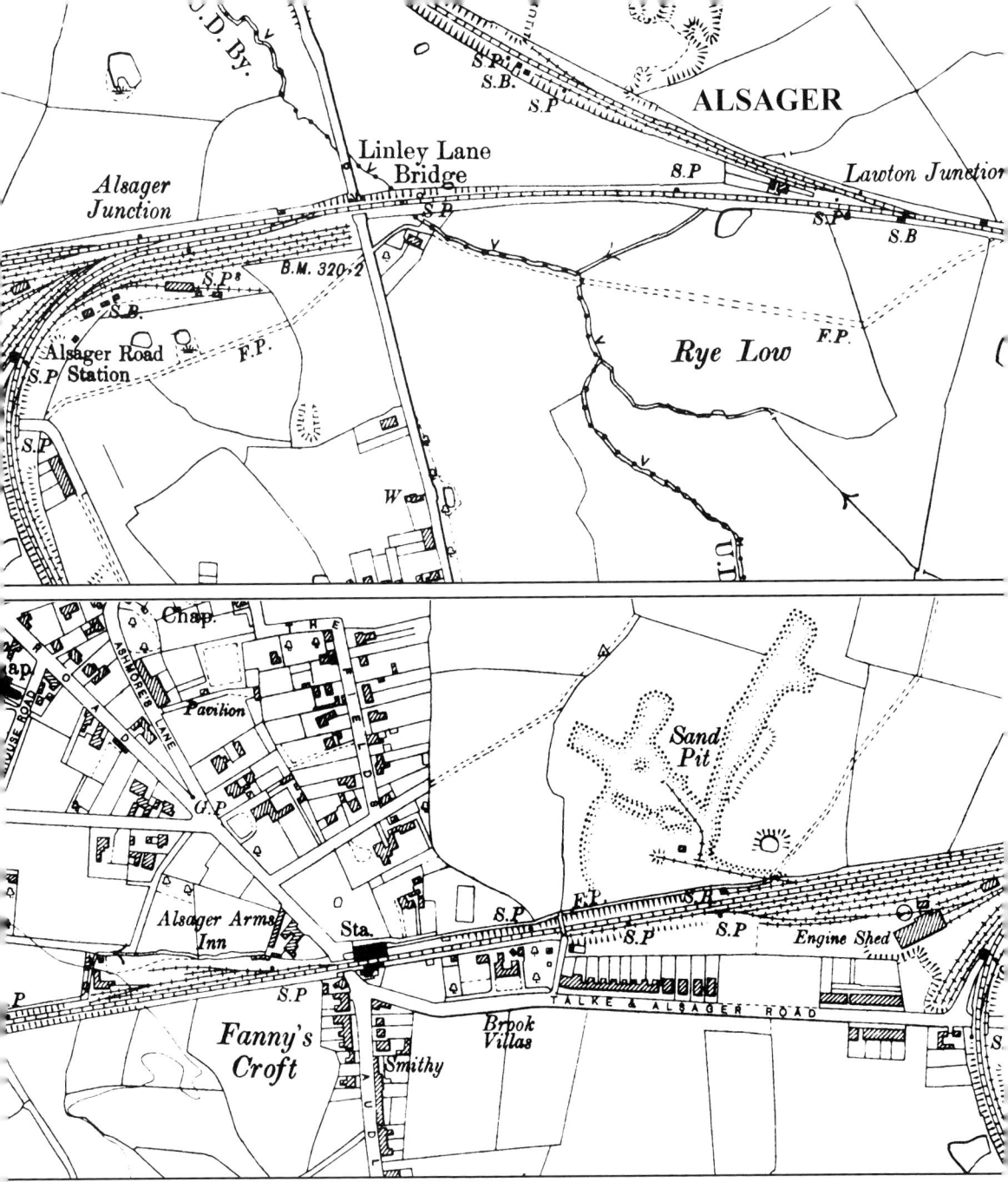

XVIII. Alsager is 2½ miles from Kidsgrove, during which our route crosses from Staffordshire into Cheshire, and descends at a ruling gradient of 1 in 100. At Lawton Junction, the Sandbach Branch diverged north westward (see pictures 77-79). Alsager Junction is shown to the left of the top section, continuing on the right of the lower section; the Audley Branch ran southward to Keele. This is featured in the Middleton Press album *Branch Lines around Market Drayton*, including Alsager Road Station. Alsager engine shed was coded 5E by the LMS and BR until its closure on 18th June 1962. The sidings at Alsager Junction were kept busy, primarily with the sorting of coal wagons, up to the late 1960s. Alsager Station was known as Alsager & Rode Heath between 1889 and 1923. The goods station, west of the passenger station, closed from 2nd November 1964. The population of Alsager Urban District rose from 2,743 in 1911 to 11,775 a century later.

65. We start with an eastward view through the station which includes the original tall signal box which served between 1872 and c1905. The box largely obscures the station house. (Railway Station Photographs)

66. This westward view from c1910 includes the replacement signal box which served until 1985. In the centre background we see the goods station, whilst the Daily News notice board is adjacent to the bookstall, which once graced the up platform. The eastern elevation of the station house is presented with a wonderful array of matching chimney stacks. (Lens of Sutton/J.Suter)

67. On 30th August 1952, class 3F 0-6-0T no. 47616 moves off the locoshed with a full bunker of coal. It is passing the coaling stage where 4MT 2-6-4T no. 42447 of Crewe North has been refuelled. (M.Dart)

68. The shed was built in 1890. It had four covered roads and other than re-roofing changed little during its 72 years of usage. After closure it stood empty until demolition c1984. On Sunday 20th March 1955, 4F 0-6-0s nos. 44452 and 44386 stand on the two more southerly roads; the former was a visitor from Burton, the latter a resident. The shed's water tank is on the right. (J.E.Bell/Transport Library)

69. The station was little changed by 13th September 1983, when class 120 DMU nos 53670, 59258 and 53744 were seen departing with the 14.34 Lincoln – Crewe, giving us a good view of the lower level version of the signal box. Progress however was not far behind. Mechanical signalling was replaced by electric colour lights controlled from Crewe in 1985 and the signal box was demolished. (A.C.Hartless)

70. An eastward view from 5th October 1985 following the end of semaphore signalling shows a hybrid DMU nos 53741, 59063 and 53652 departing with the 11.20 Crewe – Lincoln. The factory in the background belonged to Twyfords Bathrooms and closed in 2011. The prominent hill beyond it is Mow Cop (see pictures 105 - 107). Alsager Junction was located towards the end of the straight track, and the site of Alsager MPD is marked by the hump in the ground in the right background. Redundant trackwork is being lifted and the closed Alsager Yard on the left is awaiting the same treatment. In 2018 the goods loop left of the train was still in place. (A.C.Hartless)

71. The 8¼ mile Crewe Branch was electrified in 2003 enabling electric trains to run from the North West via Crewe to North Staffordshire and onto the West Midlands and London. A Euston to Crewe semi-fast service was introduced giving Alsager residents hourly through trains to the capital, although it was generally quicker to go to Crewe and catch an express. On 5th July 2018, East Midlands Trains single car DMU no. 153357 calls with the 11.07 Crewe – Derby. The NSR up side building has been replaced by a tasteful brick-built shelter, but the station house has survived in non-railway use, its canopy providing shelter on the down side. (A.C.Hartless)

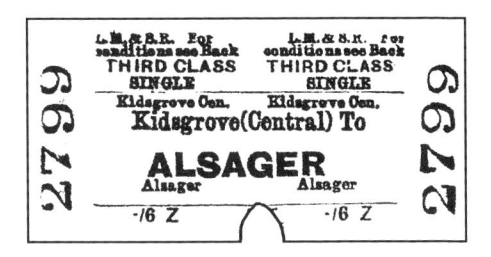

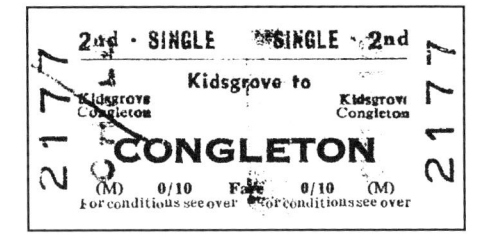

RADWAY GREEN & BARTHOLMLEY

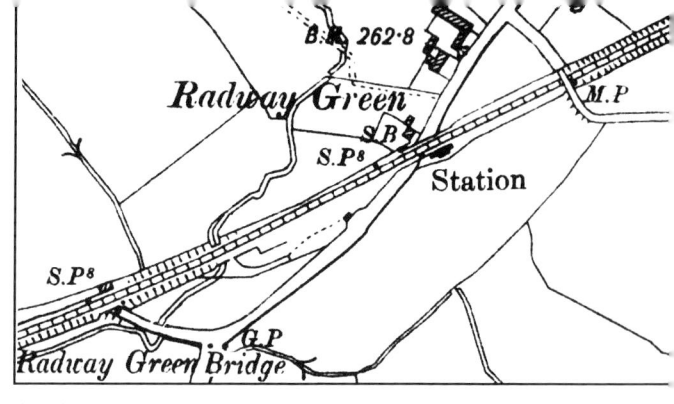

XIX. The station opened with the line as Radway Green, an agricultural hamlet 1½ miles west of Alsager. The suffix was added in 1910 for a slightly larger settlement one mile to the south. The M6 Motorway's Cheshire section opened in November 1963 and bridges the line ¼ mile west of here. The limited goods facilities closed on 6th July 1964, and passenger services were withdrawn on 7th November 1966. From ¾ miles west of here, at Bartholmley Junction, the route was reduced to a single line for 2¾ miles to the outskirts of Crewe in 1985. A significant development in 1940 was the construction of a Royal Ordnance Factory on farmland just to the east of the station on the down side. This was served by sidings which, from 1942 to 1959, incorporated an unadvertised station. This was an island platform known initially as Mill Lane and, after 1944, as Millway. It was used by workmens' trains bringing in employees from the Potteries and the Macclesfield line. The factory still produced small arms munitions in 2018.

72. This is an eastward view from an up train of the unadvertised station at Millway on 30th May 1958. A footbridge leads from the middle of the platform across sidings to the factory. Beyond the station is Radway Green Sidings signal box, which was in use between 1940 and 1967 and had 50 levers. (H.B.Oliver/Science & Society Picture Library)

73. This westward view from the occupation bridge is from about 1962. Beyond the level crossing is a solitary siding on the down side, which comprised the goods facilities. The signal box served from 1882 to 1985 and had 20 levers. (Railway Station Photographs)

CREWE

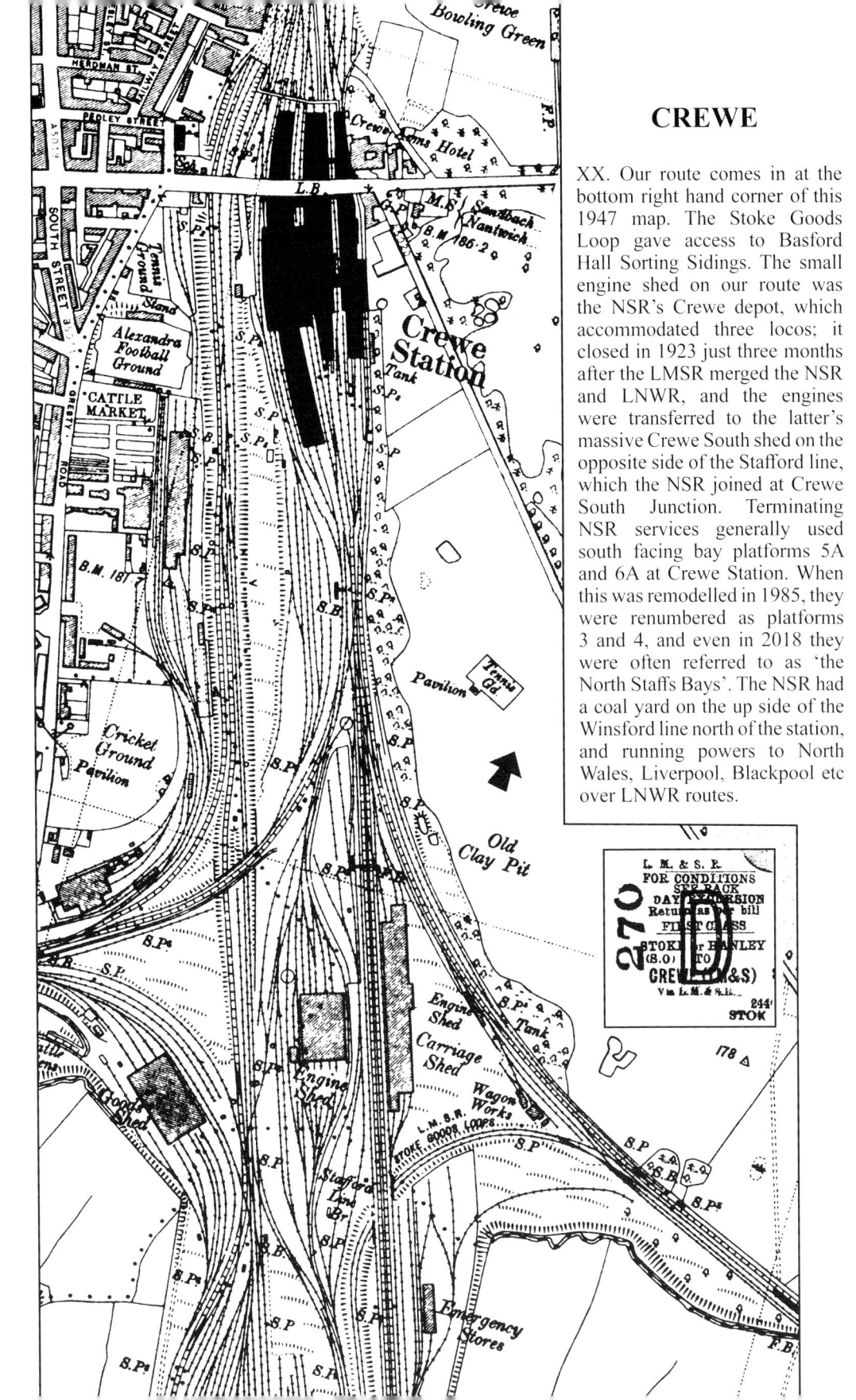

XX. Our route comes in at the bottom right hand corner of this 1947 map. The Stoke Goods Loop gave access to Basford Hall Sorting Sidings. The small engine shed on our route was the NSR's Crewe depot, which accommodated three locos; it closed in 1923 just three months after the LMSR merged the NSR and LNWR, and the engines were transferred to the latter's massive Crewe South shed on the opposite side of the Stafford line, which the NSR joined at Crewe South Junction. Terminating NSR services generally used south facing bay platforms 5A and 6A at Crewe Station. When this was remodelled in 1985, they were renumbered as platforms 3 and 4, and even in 2018 they were often referred to as 'the North Staffs Bays'. The NSR had a coal yard on the up side of the Winsford line north of the station, and running powers to North Wales, Liverpool, Blackpool etc over LNWR routes.

74. This picture shows NSR class H1 0-6-0 no. 92 coming off the Chester line of the LNWR at Crewe North Junction with a holiday special from North Wales to the Potteries. As the loco was built in early 1911 it was most likely taken before the outbreak of WW1 or in the period 1919-22 before the Grouping. (W.H.Whitworth/Real Photographs)

Further pictures of Crewe can be seen in the following albums:
Crewe to Manchester, Crewe to Wigan, Shrewsbury to Crewe **and** *Stafford to Chester.*

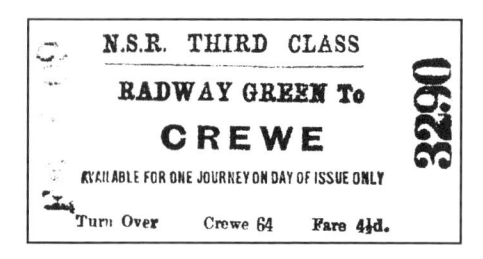

75. Class New F 0-6-4T no. 2053 stands in the North Staffs side of Crewe Station in July 1930. This loco was built in 1918 at Stoke as NSR no. 119 and ran until April 1935. (E.R.Morten/J.Suter)

76. The North Staffs side of Crewe Station is seen on 1st October 1994 as DMU no. 153325 departs from bay platform 4 with the 13.16 to Skegness, via Stoke and Derby. In 2018, bay platform 3 was generally used by the hourly London Northwestern Railway service to Euston via Stoke and Tamworth, and platform 4 by the hourly East Midlands Trains service to Stoke and Derby. (A.C.Hartless)

2. Sandbach Route

LAWTON

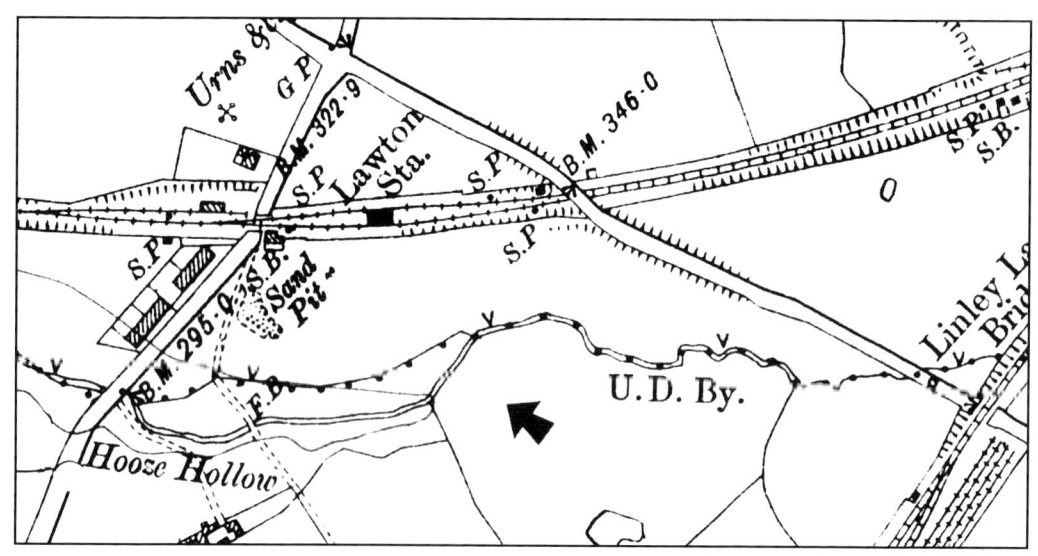

XXI. The NSR's Sandbach Branch opened in 1852 to link the local salt deposits with industrial customers in the Potteries. The passenger service was an afterthought, commencing on 3rd July 1893, and was withdrawn from 28th July 1930 during the Great Depression. The branch left the Crewe line at Lawton Junction (map XVIII), 1½ miles west of Kidsgrove. The signal box, top right, was at Lawton Sidings, and closed in 1933. Lawton Station was half a mile from Lawton Junction, on the eastern edge of Alsager. It consisted of an island platform, of which no photographs are known. The goods station was north of the passenger station and closed from 4th May 1964. The line beyond Lawton was single track. The branch closed on 4th January 1971.

77. The photographer is standing on the northern end of the station platform in this view from 1949. The box was a standard LMS design with 18 levers and served from 1927 to 1971. (Stations UK/J.Peden coll)

HASSALL GREEN

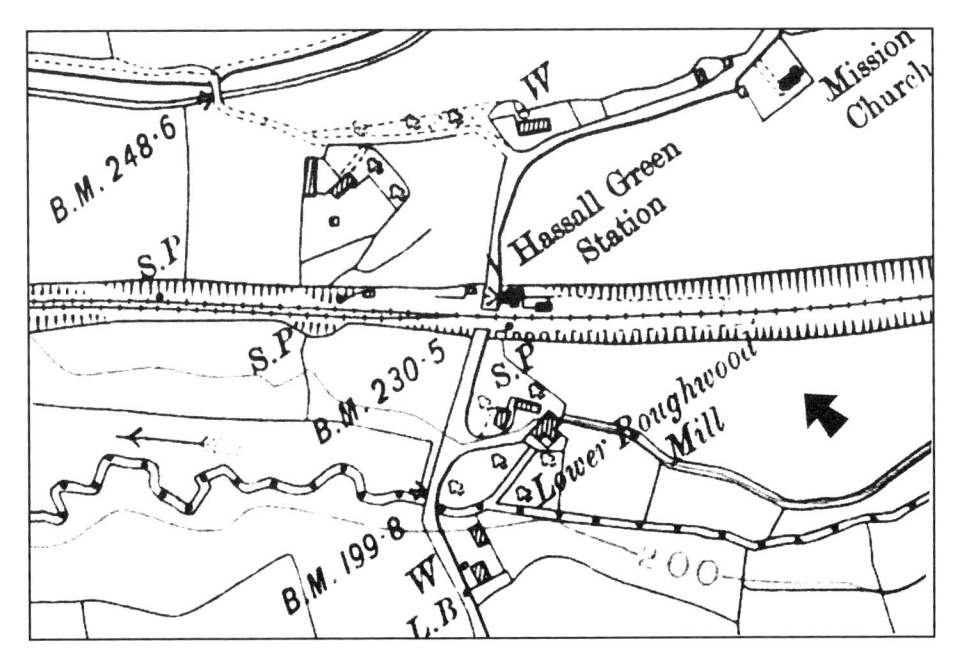

XXII. Hassall Green was 2½ miles beyond Lawton, set in quiet farming country in the Wheelock valley close to the Trent & Mersey Canal. The station opened on 17th April 1905 when Railmotors were introduced to the branch. There were limited goods facilities which ceased from 1st November 1947. Double track resumed north of the station.

78. This southward view is from the 1950s. The generous station house was separated from the single running line by the passenger platform. The signal box had 22 levers and served from 1890 to 1971. In the foreground, double track recommences towards Wheelock. (LGRP/R.Humm coll.)

WHEELOCK & SANDBACH

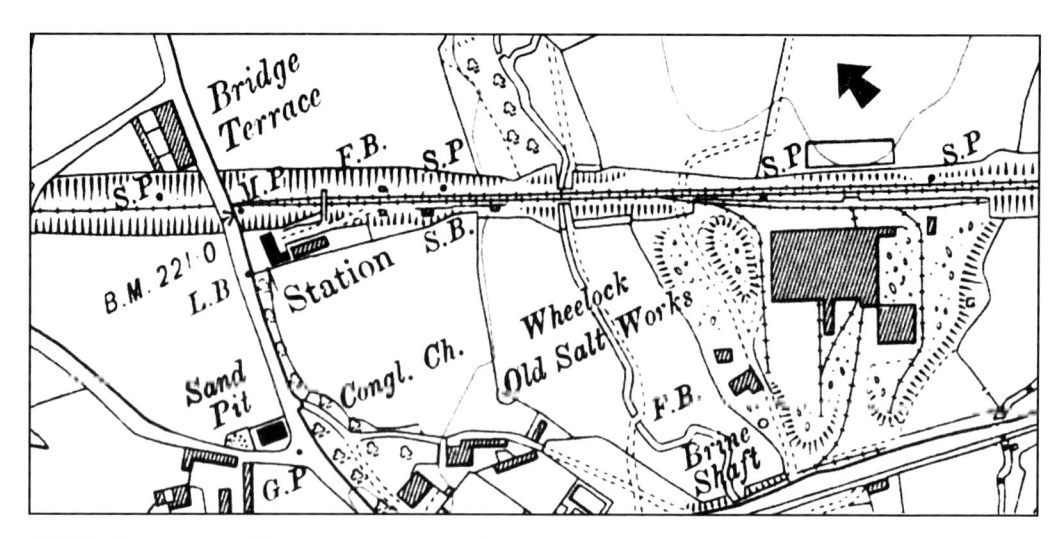

XXIII. The long-established market town of Sandbach was one mile to the north, and 1¼ miles to the east of the LNWR station. Between here and Hassall Green were rail-connected chemical works at Malkin's Bank, as well as the salt works. The branch reverted to single track beyond the station and continued to a goods station ¾ mile further on at Ettiley Heath, later known as Sandbach, which closed on 4th January 1965. The final ¾ mile link with the LNWR's Crewe – Manchester main line south of its Sandbach station did not open until the start of 1886; see picture 12 in *Crewe to Manchester*. There was never a passenger service between Wheelock NSR and Sandbach LNWR.

79. This picture appears to date from soon after the start of the passenger service. A train for Harecastle, hauled by a class D 0-6-0T, is posed at the up platform. The station house and single storey booking office at street level appear above the locomotive. A footbridge links the station entrance to the up side. Following closure the booking office was leased to commercial businesses; for many years it was a tyre depot. The signal box is on the down platform; this opened with the station and had closed by 1939. (Railway Station Photographs)

3. Etruria to Congleton

HANLEY

XXIV. The first section of what became the Potteries Loop Line opened in June 1850 as a private industrial branch from Etruria Junction to serve Earl Granville's ironworks. These were on two sites, which became Etruria Steel Works and Shelton Iron & Steel Works; the Shelton site first produced iron in 1841 and Etruria in 1853. The works came under the ownership of Shelton Bar Iron Company in 1851. Coal and ironstone were both available from the Racecourse Pits situated between the two sites; there was also an extensive brickworks. The Trent & Mersey Canal provided the means of transport for completed materials until the coming of the railway. Steel was first produced in 1888. A considerable internal railway system developed, as can be seen on the map. The run down of the site was gradual. The ironstone deposits were worked out by the mid 20th Century, and ore had then to be brought in from elsewhere. The last colliery on the site closed in 1941. As we have seen in picture 47, the last major investment was made at the Etruria site in the early 1960s. The iron and steel industry was nationalised in 1967 as the British Steel Corporation. The Shelton site was wound down rapidly thereafter and closed in 1978, and the Etruria plant ceased production in 2000. By then, activity had been limited to the western end of the site, nearest to the NSR main line. The eastern side, below Etruria Hall, was cleared in the late 1970s and early 1980s. It was used to host the National Garden Festival of 1986, celebrating the rebirth of derelict industrial land, and then became Festival Park, a landscaped mixed zone of offices, light industry and leisure activities.

The NSR's Hanley Branch was built alongside the Granville line until it took up its own course between the Etruria and Shelton Works, running south of Etruria Road to reach the town. It opened in late December 1861 for goods only. Passenger traffic commenced on 13th July 1864 to a terminus at the end of Trinity Street, which served until the Loop was extended to Burslem on 1st November 1873, whereupon a new through station was opened across the road at a lower level and on a sharp curve. The old station became the goods depot. The line climbed roughly 100ft between Etruria Junction and Hanley, a distance of around one mile, requiring a ruling gradient of 1 in 40. Hanley has long been regarded as the main commercial and cultural centre of the Potteries, but it was initially avoided by the NSR because of its hilltop position. The Loop Line was very popular in the late Victorian era, but thereafter suffered from competition from road transport. Hanley became the main hub for Potteries Motor Transport in the early 20th Century and the Loop began a terminal decline. Passenger trains ceased from 2nd March 1964, goods from 1st August 1966, and the line closed entirely on 31st July 1969.

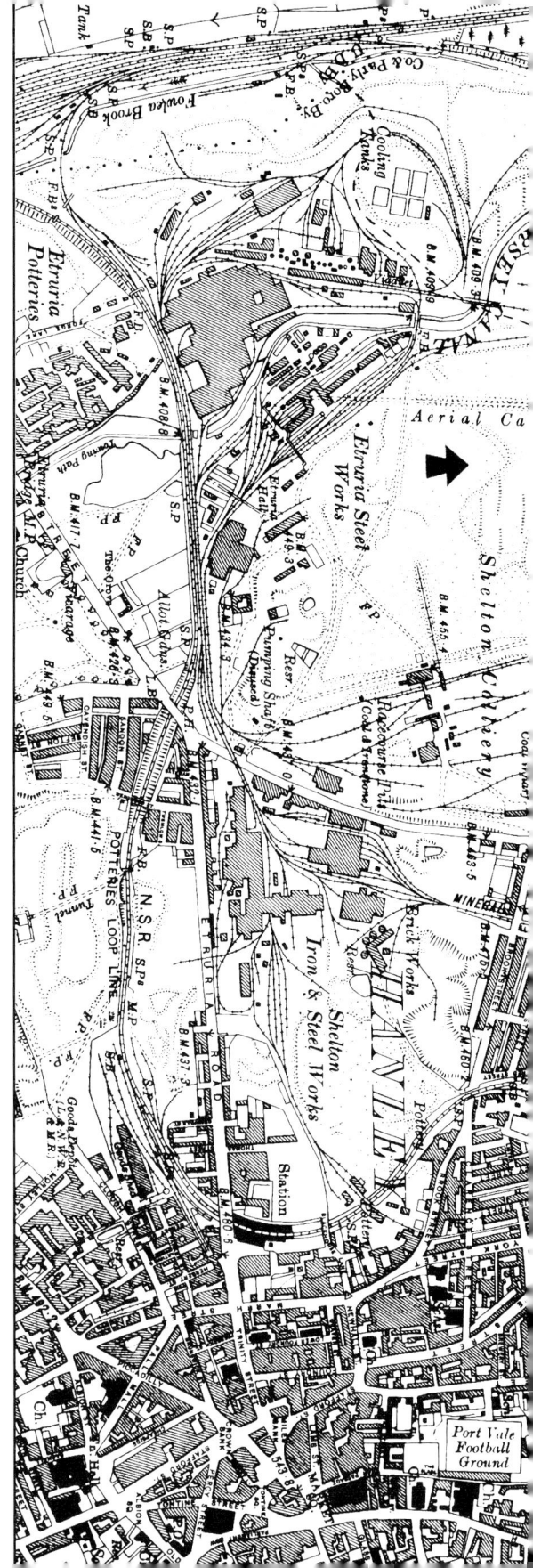

80. A northward view from 12th June 1948 shows 4MT 2-6-4T no. 42676 with an up Loop Line service of three coaches. The loco is carrying its British Railways number but the owner is still shown as LMS. Close inspection of the platform canopies reveals unrepaired damage from WW2. (W.A.Camwell/SLS)

81. This view of the exterior of Hanley Station dates from c1950. The limited car parking spaces are on offer at 1/- per day. Note the BR truck on the right; parcels continued to be dealt with here until mid-1970, 12 months after the line was closed. (R.Humm coll.)

HANLEY,
A telegraph station.
Containing a population of 31,953 inhabitants, is a municipal borough in the north of Staffordshire. The iron trade is now becoming a most important feature in the commerce of the pottery district. Earl Granville's furnaces, located near Hanley, employ about 3,000 hands.
To the north of Hanley is *Norton-in-the-Moors*. These moors stretch for miles and miles through this end of the county, into Derbyshire and Yorkshire.

Bradshaw Guide, 1866.

82. This is the Etruria Steel Works in about 1950. We are looking roughly north-north eastwards. The Loop Line comes in lower left and leaves at the right where it crosses the Trent & Mersey Canal. Below the Loop is the Etruria Works of Josiah Wedgwood; this was in the process of closure, having recently been replaced by a new factory at Barlaston. The steelworks takes up the remainder of the picture, with the canal snaking through the view before disappearing into the distance. The scale of the internal railway system is apparent from the number of sidings and wagons. The new steelworks which opened in 1964 was built on the mostly vacant ground at the left. In 2018, the canal was all that remained of this view. (A.C.Hartless coll.)

83. The steelworks had a fleet of around 20 shunting locos. Diesels began to replace steam in the early 1950s and reigned supreme by the early 70s. The last steamer to leave was the 0-4-0 crane tank, Dubs no. 4101 of 1901, which was preserved in 1973 and which in 2018 could be found at the Foxfield Railway. Here it is seen at Shelton on 28th May 1955. (J.Faithfull/RCTS)

84. By the time of this picture, 26th March 1963, traffic on the Loop Line had dwindled markedly, and there were long periods of quiet between the morning and evening peaks. The view is towards Etruria. The station building, modest at street level, towers above the up side platform. Note the replacement canopies, much shorter than their predecessors, the concrete lamp posts, and the check rails; the curvature prevented the use of BR Mk 1 coaching stock. In the early 1970s the site was filled and levelled to street height, where the photographer is standing. (R.Humm coll.)

85. The steelworks outlived the Loop Line by over 30 years, accessed as we have seen earlier from the Grange Branch. A freight photo charter took place on 18th March 1995, using two preserved industrial steam locos from the Foxfield Light Rly. On the embankment is *Robert Heath* no. 6 (see also picture 117), and on the low level line is Wm Bagnall 0-4-0ST *Hawarden*. This was works number 2623 of 1940 and was the last built of the 30 or so steam locos known to have worked at Shelton Bar. It left the steelworks in 1972 for preservation. (T.Heavyside)

XXV. This overlaps map XXIV; Waterloo Road was only 30 chains from Hanley. It was the penultimate station on the Loop Line to open, on 1st April 1900, and the first to close, from 4th October 1943. Waterloo Road is the main road between Hanley and Burslem and road competition soon overcame the less frequent train service. Potteries Electric Traction operated trams along 32 miles of route by 1904, including the length of Waterloo Road, and first used motor buses in 1900. When tram operation ended in 1928 the company was renamed Potteries Motor Traction. North of the station were exchange sidings and a spur to Shelton Steel's branch line to Shelton Colliery Deep Pits, aka Hanley Deep Pit, which closed in 1962. The branch crossed Waterloo Road on the level, and the Loop Line as that was entering Cobridge Tunnel, which was 300 yards long and with an adverse gradient northbound of 1 in 67.

86. This post closure view from the 1950s is the only one of which we are aware. We are looking back from a southbound train. The booking office straddling the line is still intact, but the platforms are clearly disused. The sidings on the right were principally used by W. Walker & Sons, distributors of fuel oil. The line beyond closed on 3rd January 1966 as far as Goldenhill. (H.B.Oliver/R.Humm coll.)

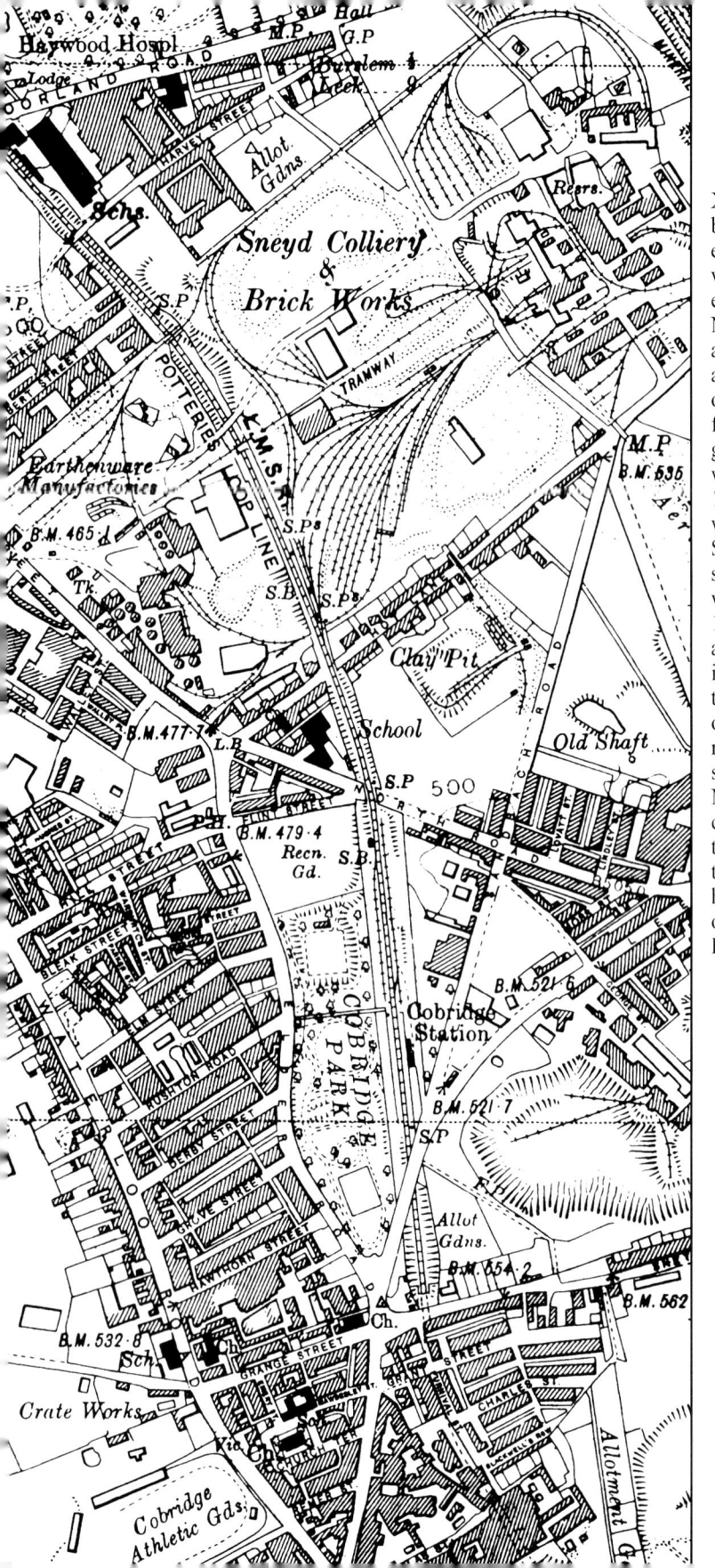

COBRIDGE

XXVI. Our route runs from bottom to top on this 1947 edition. Cobridge opened with the Hanley to Burslem extension of the line on 1st November 1873. It was half a mile from Waterloo Road and just beyond the summit of an almost continual climb from Etruria. It had limited goods facilities which closed with the line from 1st August 1966. The immediate district was mostly residential, but Sneyd Colliery was only a short distance away. This was in production from the 1820s until 1962, when, as with Hanley Deep Pit, it was linked underground to Wolstanton and surface operations ceased. It is remembered for a disastrous subterranean explosion on New Year's Day 1942 which cost 57 lives. The track bed of the Loop Line from Cobridge to Kidsgrove Market Street has been utilised as part of National Cycle Path 5, Reading to Holyhead.

87. This is an early 1950s view of the up platform. The buildings were of timber construction. Sandbach Road crosses the line at an oblique angle at the far right.
(Railway Station Photographs)

88. Looking north from Sandbach Road on 28th May 1960, we see the neat and tidy station in the clear light of a spring day. Note the barrow crossing at the far end of the platforms, and the sidings beyond, one on each side, which served as the goods station. Beyond Cobridge signal box, which served throughout the life of the line, the tracks curve leftwards towards Burslem. Sneyd Colliery occupies the mid-ground, with more wagons than it is possible to count. The floodlights of Vale Park, Port Vale FC's home from 1950, can be seen above the down side shelter. (H.B.Priestley/R.Humm coll.)

89. Sneyd Colliery was situated on a hillside and there was severe curvature in places. This called for an articulated Beyer-Garratt 0-4-4-0T, one of only a handful built for domestic industrial use. It bore the name *Sneyd Collieries No. 3*, and was in use from 1931 until the pit's closure, after which it was sadly scrapped. The picture is dated 19th May 1962, shortly before it was retired. (J.Faithfull/RCTS)

BURSLEM

XXVII. The map overlaps the previous one; the distance from Cobridge was a little under ¾ mile. Burslem is generally acknowledged to be the oldest of the Potteries' six towns; it was a centre for pottery manufacture as long ago as the 12th century. The railway was built to the east of Market Place. There was a small goods station which closed from 9th October 1961. Note also Grange Wharf lower right; this was the terminus of the Grange Branch from Etruria (map XIV), which closed from 3rd April 1950.

90. A view from the 1900s shows a down Loop Line service departing northward. The locomotive is partially obscured by the signal box, whilst the carriages are six-wheeled non-compartment stock, typical of local services of this era. The goods station is in the foreground with several horses going about their business; the nearest MR wagon appears to be loaded with beer barrels, either full from Burton, or empty on their way thence. (Railway Station Photographs)

91. On 28th May 1960, a BRCW three-coach unit led by power car no. M50424, comes under Hamil Road with the 1.50pm (SO) Macclesfield – Stoke. The signal box had 20 levers and was open from 1879 until 1963. Note the NSR running in board on the right. (H.B.Priestley/R.Humm coll.)

92. This southward view appears to date from after the closure of the good facilities but before that of the signal box. The booking office is the solid looking building with three windows at the top of the drive on the right-hand side. This largely obscures the public baths beyond. An inbound PMT bus crosses the railway, having just passed the twin gables of Moorland Road School; above the bus can be seen the faint conical outline of Sneyd Colliery's spoil tip. (A.Field/R.Humm coll.)

BURSLEM.

POPULATION, 17,821.
Distance from station, ¾ mile.
A telegraph station.
HOTEL.—Leopard.
MARKET DAYS.—Monday and Saturday.
FAIRS.—Saturday before Shrove Sunday, Easter Day, Whit Sunday (the only place in England where a fair is held on a Sunday), Midsummer Day, day after Christmas.

In old times, Burslem was noted for its common yellow ware, so much so that "Butter Pot" was its ordinary name, even on the county map. Near here Josiah Wedgwood was born in 1730, and brought his improved wares and porcelain to perfection; but the china clay, felspar or soapstone, and flint, necessary for the finer sorts, are imported from the south, especially Devonshire and Cornwall.

Bradshaw Guide, 1866.

TUNSTALL

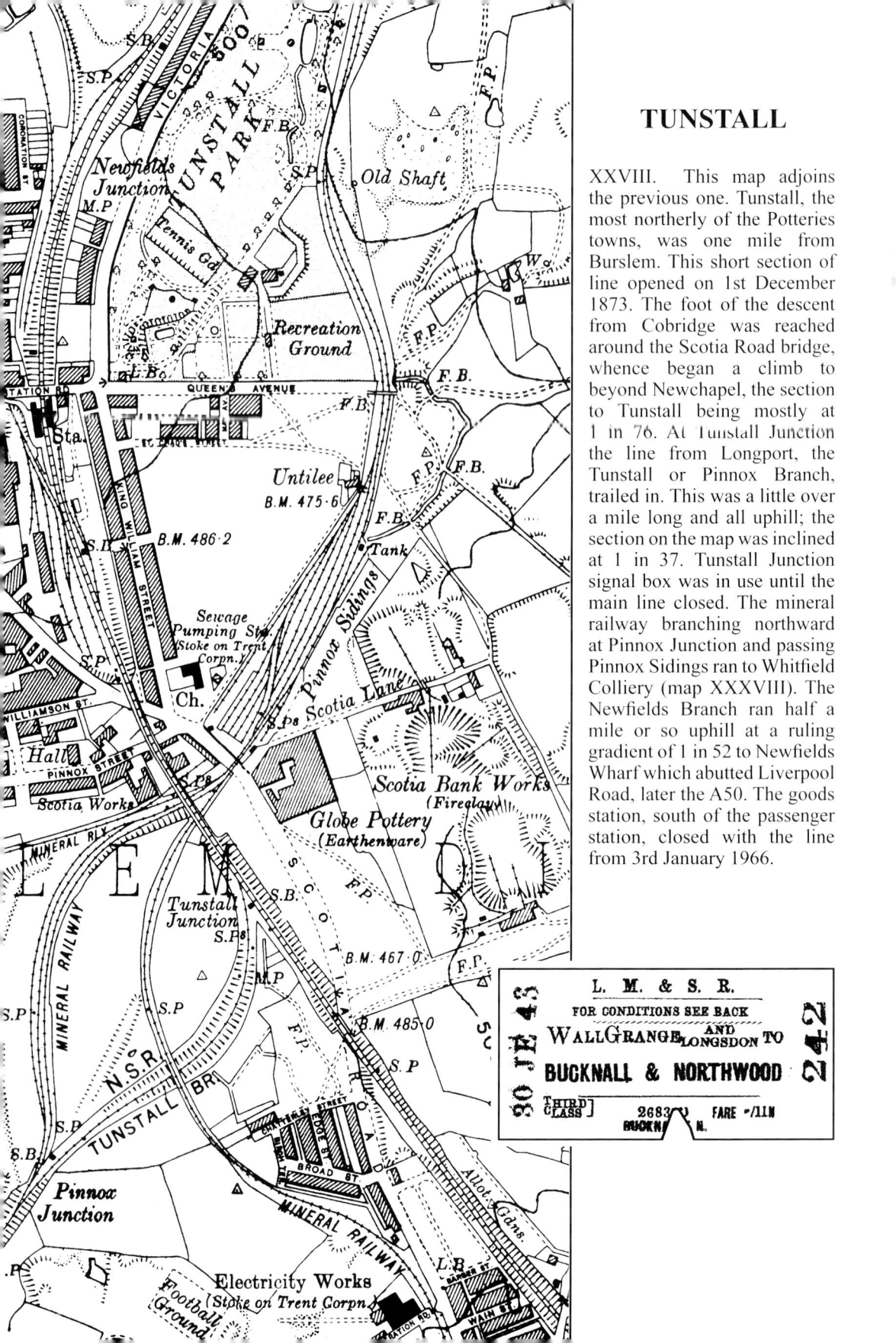

XXVIII. This map adjoins the previous one. Tunstall, the most northerly of the Potteries towns, was one mile from Burslem. This short section of line opened on 1st December 1873. The foot of the descent from Cobridge was reached around the Scotia Road bridge, whence began a climb to beyond Newchapel, the section to Tunstall being mostly at 1 in 76. At Tunstall Junction the line from Longport, the Tunstall or Pinnox Branch, trailed in. This was a little over a mile long and all uphill; the section on the map was inclined at 1 in 37. Tunstall Junction signal box was in use until the main line closed. The mineral railway branching northward at Pinnox Junction and passing Pinnox Sidings ran to Whitfield Colliery (map XXXVIII). The Newfields Branch ran half a mile or so uphill at a ruling gradient of 1 in 52 to Newfields Wharf which abutted Liverpool Road, later the A50. The goods station, south of the passenger station, closed with the line from 3rd January 1966.

93. This is a northward view of the station in around 1950. There was a marked similarity in the footbridges here and at Burslem; both were installed in 1938.
(NSR Study Group)

94. This poor quality undated print looks southward along the goods yard headshunt. The rear of the down side station building is on the left. In the centre is Tunstall Station signal box, which had 24 levers and served from 1878 until the line closed. Centre right is the commodious goods station, where what appears to be a 4F 0-6-0 is shunting. (NSR Study Group)

95. On 29th June 1953 ex-LNWR 'Cauliflower' 0-6-0 BR no. 58382 has arrived at Tunstall from the south with the daily Newfields goods. Stoke shed had a few of these ancient locos, the heaviest permitted on the Newfields Branch, which closed from 3rd August 1959.
(F.W.Shuttleworth)

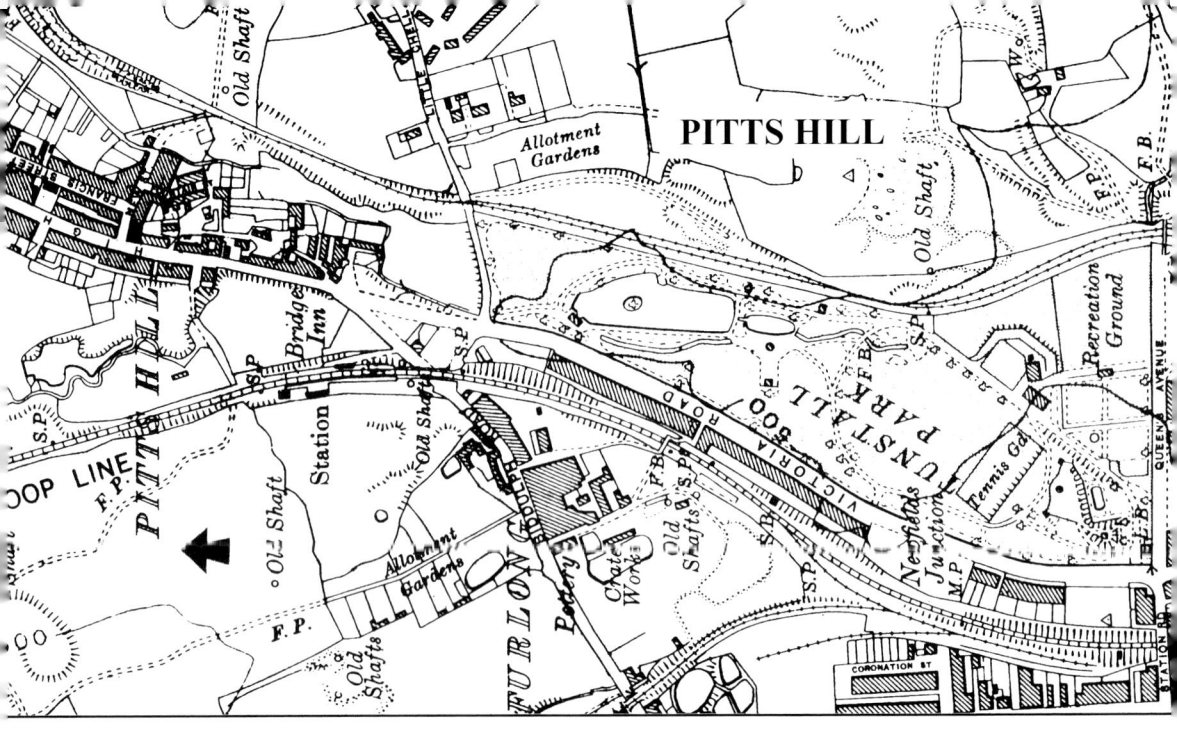

XXIX. Pitts Hill was a little over half a mile beyond Tunstall, all uphill with a ruling gradient of 1 in 76. The station opened on 1st October 1874 with the Loop Line extension from Tunstall to Newchapel. There was no goods station. The Whitfield Colliery to Pinnox Junction mineral line runs roughly parallel to our route.

96. On 21st August 1958 a BRCW DMU arrives with a Stoke – Congleton working. The station presents a tidy appearance including recently installed BR LMR signage. Greenfield Pottery dominates the right background. (H.B.Oliver/Science & Society Picture Library)

97. This northward view of the station was taken in May 1964, some 10 weeks post closure. Signs and benches have been removed, but otherwise the station is still intact. It can be seen that the main buildings were on the down side, comprising a single storey booking office cum waiting room and the station masters house, beyond the platform. Subsequent development has obliterated the site. (B.Bentley/Stoke-on-Trent City Archive)

98. On Saturday 13th March 1965, Manchester University Railway Society's 'The Staffordshire Potter' rail tour covered all the lines in this book (except for Leek – Leekbrook Jn and Lawton Jn – Crewe), also the Caldon Low branch and other lines in Cheshire and Manchester. The locomotive for the day was Fowler class 4 2-6-4T no. 42343, a former Stoke resident now shedded at Stockport, and which was withdrawn seven months later. Here the special is seen running south from the end of the down platform. (RailOnline)

NEWCHAPEL & GOLDENHILL

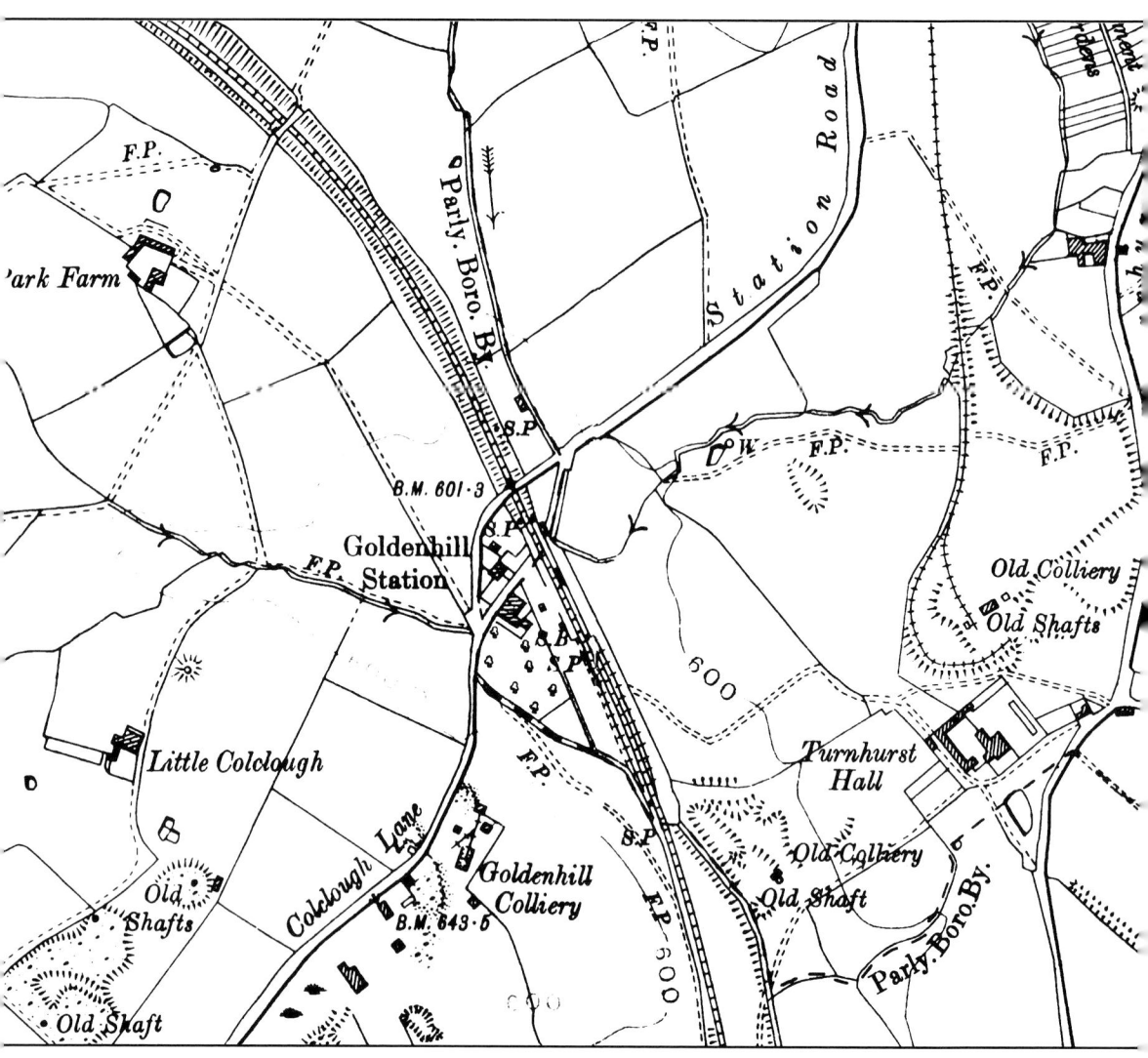

XXX. The Loop Line was extended here from Tunstall on 1st October 1874. The station was known simply as Goldenhill until the start of 1913. It was one mile from Pitts Hill, once again uphill northbound, mostly at 1 in 148. Goldenhill was ½ mile southward along Colclough Lane, Newchapel was ½ mile in the opposite direction. There was a goods siding which closed with the passenger station from 2nd March 1964.

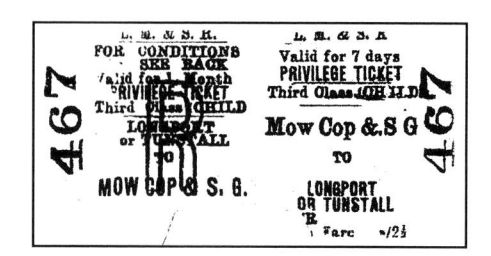

99. We look north from the down platform sometime in the early 1950s and notice that the only platform buildings were on the up side. There is a trailing crossover beneath Colclough Lane bridge; certain trains terminated here. The line continues to climb into the distance. The route was singled as early as 1909 from 7 chains north of the station to Kidsgrove. (Railway Station Photographs)

100. A southerly view from the bridge on 12th April 1962 illustrates the limited facilities, also the bleakness of the location. Just off the up platform is the lamp room, adjacent to a well-trodden boarded crossing. A fire is burning in the waiting room. The signal box is at the end of the up platform with another crossing close by. The box had just 14 levers and was in use from 1880 until the line closed at the start of 1966. Beyond are sidings both sides of the line, but neither has any wagons. The change of gradient marker right foreground shows a stiffening of the gradient for down trains, to 1 in 105 for the last stretch of the climb to the summit.
(F.W.Shutttleworth/Railway Station Photographs)

XXXI. The Goldenhill to Kidsgrove line opened on 15th November 1875, the last link in the Potteries Loop. It runs from right to left of the map as it turns westward. The Weaver/Trent watershed marked the summit of the Loop Line at around 610ft above sea level. The Urban District boundary shortly afterwards was the northern limit of the City of Stoke-on-Trent. From here the line fell precipitously at 1 in 40 to Kidsgrove Halt, also known as Kidsgrove Market Street Halt, which was a little less than 1½ miles from Newchapel & Goldenhill. For most of this section, the line passed through the site of Birchenwood Ironworks, which was in production between 1833 and 1891. It was replaced by a major coking and by-products plant, the main product of which was coal gas. It lasted until 1973

101. This was the halt in a 1930s view looking towards Newchapel & Goldenhill. A grounded body from a Victorian era railway carriage forms the middle of the three timber buildings. The nearer track was part of the Birchenwood internal system which ran parallel to the single Loop Line. Note the running in board reads simply 'Kidsgrove'. (Science & Society Picture Library)

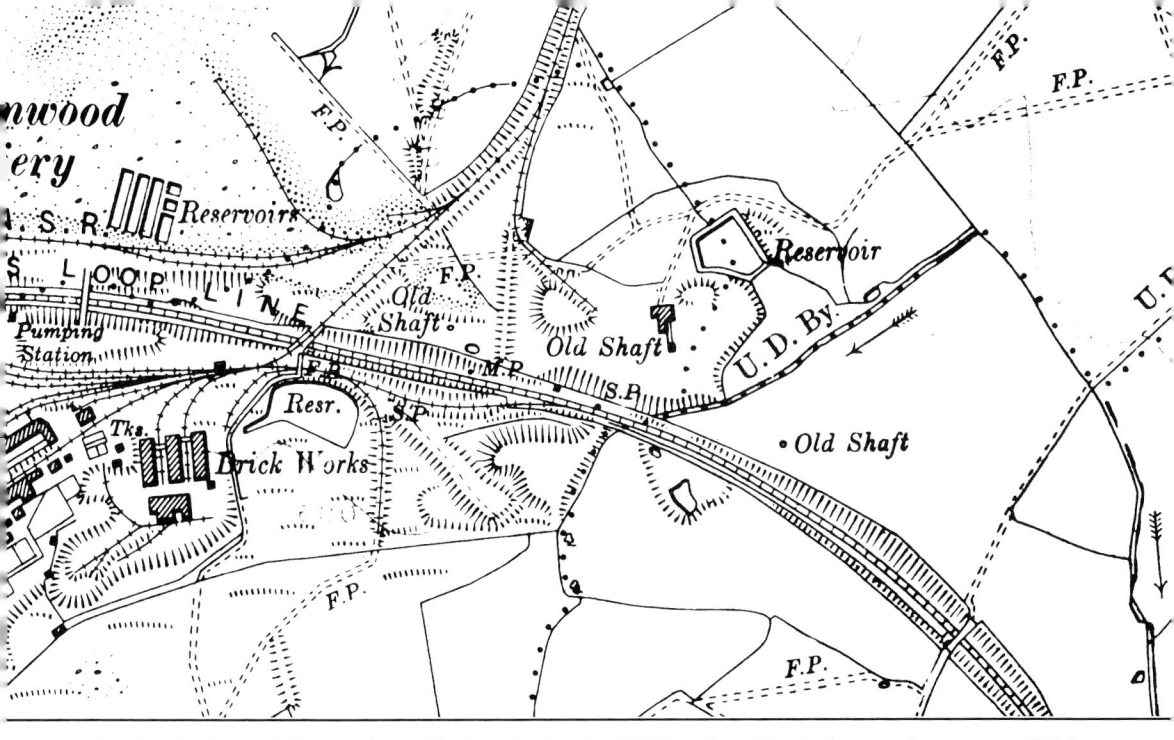

(despite the last of the on-site collieries closing in 1931), when North Sea gas became available. The line coming in at the right upper margin was a mineral line linking Birchenwood to Biddulph Ironworks and Victoria Colliery. The halt was close to the cinema to the left of the map. It opened on 1st July 1909 when the line from Goldenhill was singled, so that only one platform was required. In LMS days southbound trains ceased to call because of the adverse gradient, and it closed entirely from 25th September 1950. The Loop Line closed to all traffic from 3rd January 1966, but the section from Newchapel & Goldenhill to Kidsgrove was retained for opencast coal traffic, which ran between 1970 and early 1976 from a loading point called Park Farm, near the summit.

102. Birchenwood retained two steam locos for shunting until the works closed in mid-1973, becoming the last industrial location in North Staffordshire to use steam. Large Peckett 0-6-0ST no. 2153 came here new in 1954 and is seen in the works on 31st August 1972. It was purchased for preservation on its withdrawal, and in 2018 could be found on the Caledonian Railway in Brechin. (A.C.Hartless)

KIDSGROVE LIVERPOOL ROAD

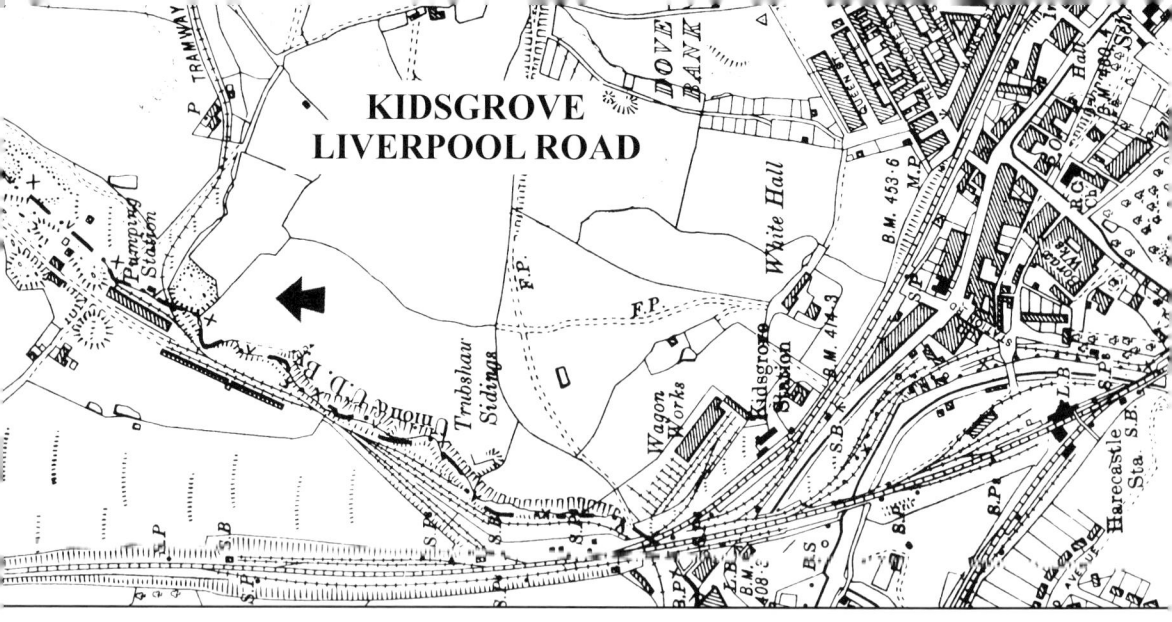

XXXII. This map overlaps with numbers XVII and XXXI. Our route comes in at the top right. The station opened with the final section of the Loop Line from Goldenhill. It was half a mile from Market Street Halt and was called simply Kidsgrove until 2nd October 1944. There was no goods station owing to the close proximity of Harecastle. The local topography made it impossible to create a junction between the Loop Line and the main line south of Harecastle station. The Loop therefore joined the Macclesfield line at Kidsgrove Junction, facing north. Trubshaw Sidings were on the site of Harecastle Colliery, which closed in 1897. The signal box marked below Kidsgrove Station was called Kidsgrove and was in operation from 1879 to 1934. Kidsgrove Junction box did not open until 1917. It had 82 levers, which were reduced to 25 in 1965 when it was downgraded to a shunting frame and halved in length. It served in this capacity for another 20 years. The box at the bottom left of the map was Harecastle North, which was in use from 1879 to 1935.

103. This eastward view was dated 23rd August 1957. The up side booking office and waiting rooms were placed some distance behind the platform, at the far end of which a ticket inspector's cubicle marks the entrance. Single track commenced around the bend beyond the platforms. The Birchenwood line disappears behind the down platform where it had a small yard for the transfer of traffic with the main line. (H.B.Oliver/ Science & Society Picture Library)

104. Looking west on 26th September 1960, we see the late afternoon Crewe Works-Stoke workmens' train behind class 4MT 2-6-4T no. 42668. This has arrived from the Crewe Branch at Kidsgrove Central, reversed along the Macclesfield line, then drawn forward at Kidsgrove Junction, whose signal box is visible in the background. Note the water tank at the far end of the down platform. (M.Mensing)

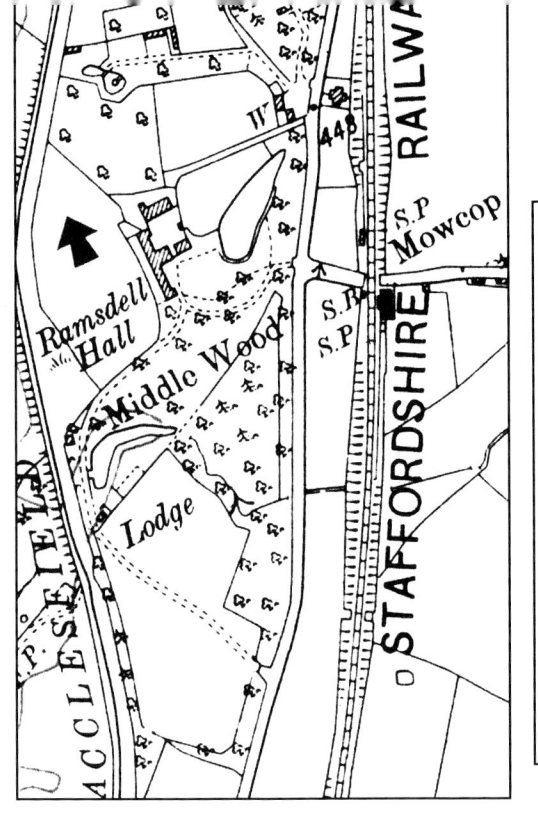

MOW COP & SCHOLAR GREEN

MOW COP.

Distance from station, 1½ mile.
Telegraph station at Kidsgrove, 2½ miles.
MONEY ORDER OFFICE at Congleton.

Mow Cop is a mountain in miniature, precipitous on three sides, bleak, bare, and craggy, except in one part, where there is a fine hanging wood. From the summit of this hill, 1,091 feet high, the finest views imaginable are obtainable in every direction. In certain states of the atmosphere, it is said, that the shipping beyond the port of Liverpool are distinguishable. The Welsh mountains, the Wrekin in Shropshire, Beeston Castle, the Peak of Derbyshire, and the lofty range of hills which form the Staffordshire moorlands, are prominent objects. Nearer, on the south, almost the whole of the Pottery district is seen. Congleton lies nearer still to the north. The whole country northward is studded over with towns and villages, of which a sort of bird's-eye glance is presented. But nothing can be more glorious than the view from it of almost the entire county of Chester. The hill stands on the boundary line between the counties of Stafford and Chester. On the summit there is an artificial ruin, which has a good appearance in every point of view.

Bradshaw Guide, 1866.

XXXIII. Mow Cop was 2¼ miles down the NSR main line from Harecastle and appears to have opened six months or so after the line, around June 1849. The suffix was added in the mid-1890s. Mow Cop, Staffs, is the name of both a steep hill 1,100 feet high one mile to the east and the village thereon which grew around its stone quarries; Scholar Green, Cheshire, is one mile to the south west on the Newcastle to Congleton road. The Macclesfield Canal, linking Kidsgrove and Marple, was one of the last canals to be built, opening in 1831. Goods facilities were withdrawn from the station from 1st June 1939, and passenger services ceased from 7th September 1964.

105. We start with an Edwardian postcard view northwards with half a dozen figures neatly posed. The platforms are staggered either side of the lane, which rightward rises sharply up the hill. The track here is level, following the very eastern edge of the Cheshire Plain. The down platform shows evidence of an extension. (R.Humm coll.)

106. A similar view from 29th August 1957 indicates no significant change in the intervening 50 or so years, although a bike shed has been added at the far right. We get a better view of the main building, incorporating the station masters house, on the up side. What looks like a class 2MT 2-6-0 with a short train of loaded ballast wagons heads south. (H.B.Priestley/R.Humm coll.)

107. On the same day, the down 'Comet' express from Euston to Manchester London Road runs past behind a pair of mixed traffic class 5 4-6-0s instead of the usual 'Royal Scot' class; the pilot loco is no. 44938. Note the separate pedestrian crossing gates in the left foreground, also the lane to Scholar Green between the train and the signal box. The box was in use between 1879 and 2002; it had just 14 levers until the frame was replaced by switches in 1981. (H.B.Priestley/R.Humm coll.)

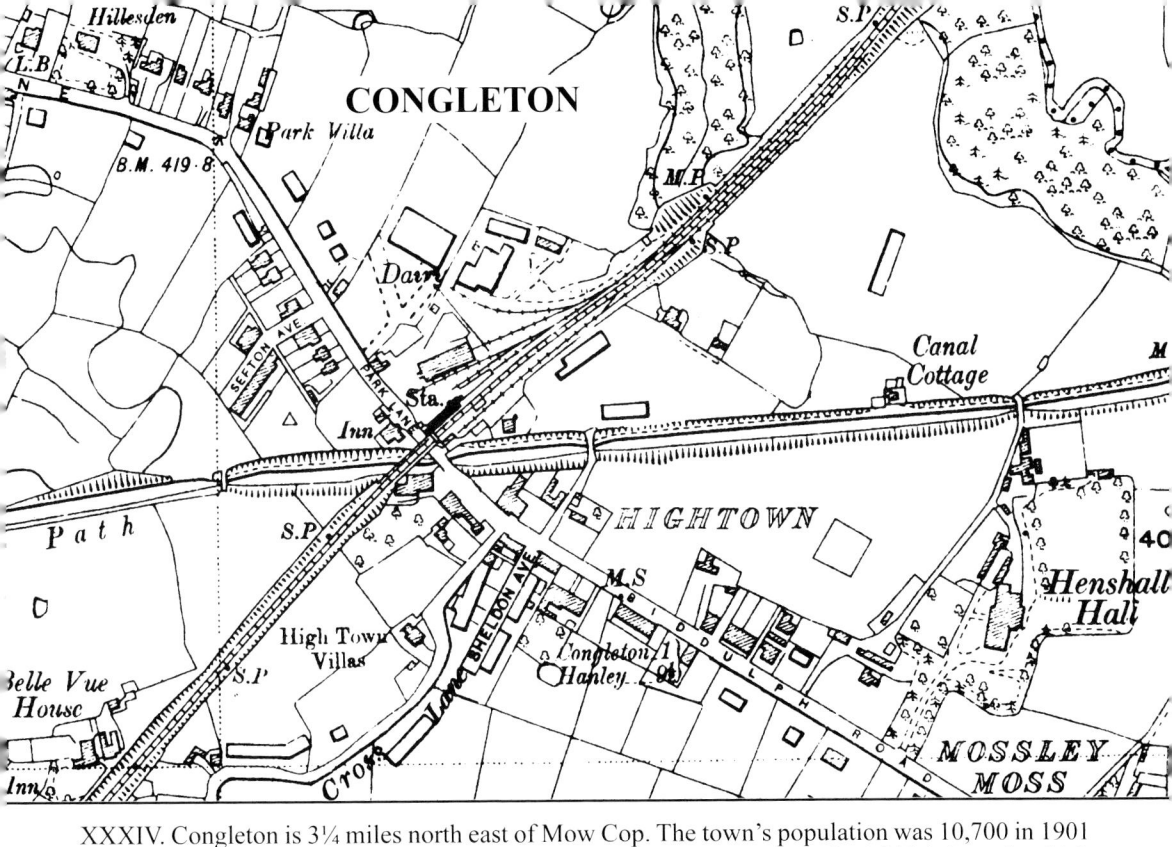

XXXIV. Congleton is 3¼ miles north east of Mow Cop. The town's population was 10,700 in 1901 and 26,480 in 2011. The station is ¾ mile east of the town centre on the Biddulph road, which was crossed on the level close to where the road bridged the Macclesfield Canal. The station was completely rebuilt in the mid-1960s when the line was electrified and the level crossing was replaced by a bridge. The goods station remained open until the end of 1976, and the warehouse was used afterwards as a permanent way store. Beyond Congleton, the NSR main line continues to North Rode, 3¼ miles to the north, and Macclesfield. These are illustrated in *Uttoxeter to Macclesfield*.

108. This early picture, probably from the 1890s, looks northward through the station and captures the rear of a goods train. The level crossing is in the foreground with a keepers hut at the far left. The tall 26 lever signal box, in use from 1870 – 1964, partially obscures the main station building on the down side, however we can see examples of decorative brickwork, typical of NSR buildings of the late 1840s, on both platforms. The line has been deemed sufficiently busy to merit a footbridge. Note at this date the absence of an up starting signal. (R.Humm coll.)

109. This undated southward view appears to be from the early 1950s. The bicycle shed is a relatively recent addition on the down side. The goods station was on the down side, out of view, but there were also a couple of sidings on the up side, the nearer of which was originally the bay platform for Biddulph Valley services. The mill in the background belonged to the Oakes family, suppliers of animal feedstuffs since 1675. (Railway Station Photographs)

110. This exterior view from June 1954 shows the main building to good advantage and gives us an idea of the fine architectural details the NSR incorporated into its larger stations. The flat-roofed single-storey section in the centre appears to be a later but sympathetic addition. The wagons, far left, mark the southern end of the goods yard. In the distance, Congleton Cloud, 1,125ft above sea level, marks the northern end of the ridge of hills running from the Potteries. (H.Jack/R.Humm coll.)

111. This picture was taken from around the same spot as no. 109 on 5th July 2018 and shows a CrossCountry Voyager hurrying past with the 07.30 Bournemouth – Manchester Piccadilly. The station appears as it was rebuilt in the mid-1960s with the addition of a waiting shelter on each platform. There is little to link the two views, although close inspection reveals Oakes's mill on the left, largely obscured by tree growth. (A.C.Hartless)

4. Biddulph Route
NORTH OF CONGLETON

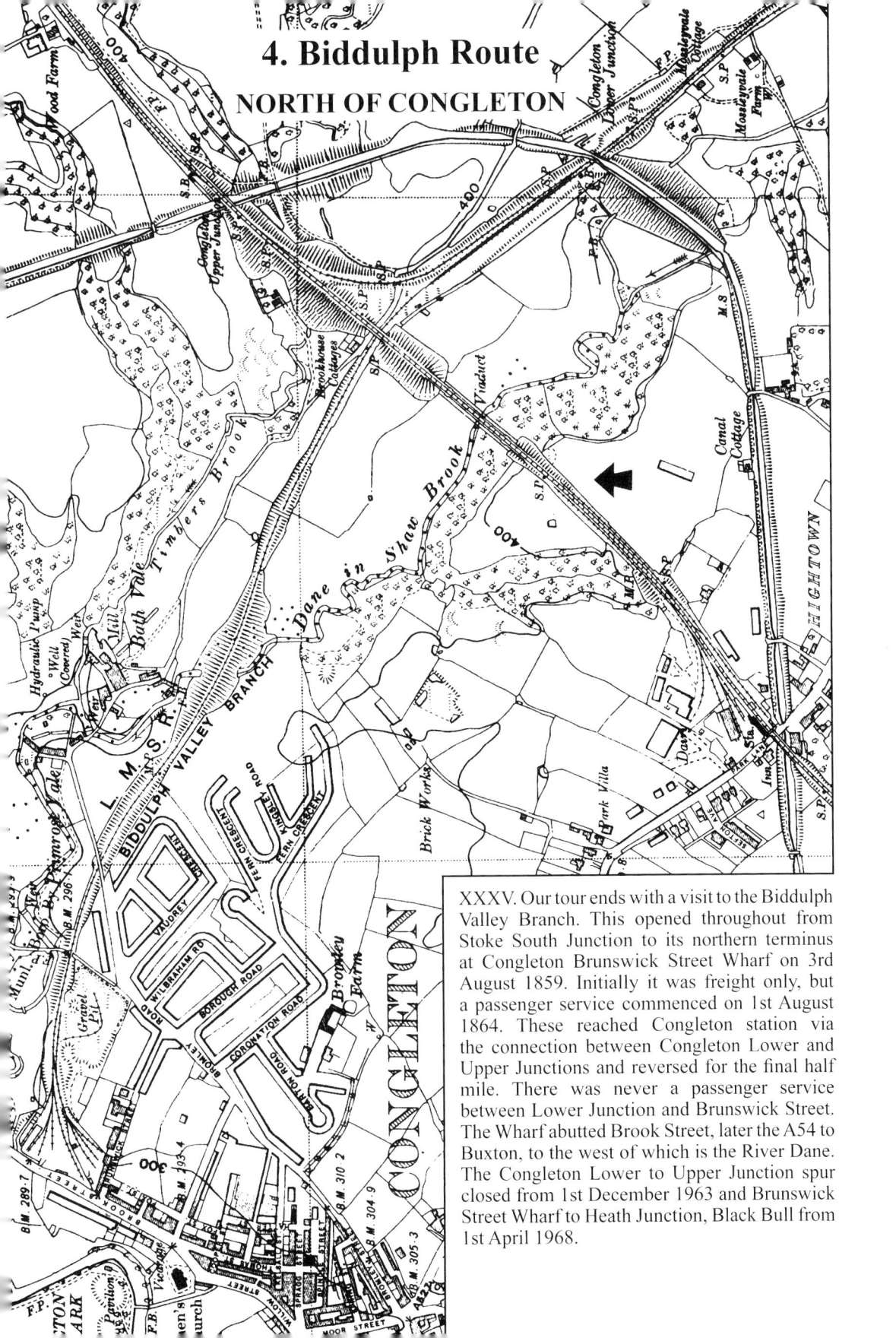

XXXV. Our tour ends with a visit to the Biddulph Valley Branch. This opened throughout from Stoke South Junction to its northern terminus at Congleton Brunswick Street Wharf on 3rd August 1859. Initially it was freight only, but a passenger service commenced on 1st August 1864. These reached Congleton station via the connection between Congleton Lower and Upper Junctions and reversed for the final half mile. There was never a passenger service between Lower Junction and Brunswick Street. The Wharf abutted Brook Street, later the A54 to Buxton, to the west of which is the River Dane. The Congleton Lower to Upper Junction spur closed from 1st December 1963 and Brunswick Street Wharf to Heath Junction, Black Bull from 1st April 1968.

112. Manchester University Railway Society's 'The Staffordshire Potter' rail tour on Saturday 13th March 1965 is seen for a second time (see picture no. 98). In this view of the normally goods only Brunswick Wharf, we look towards the end of the line and get a glimpse of the facilities, particularly the large shed, where goods were transferred between rail and road. One regular commodity of note was locally quarried sand which was taken by train to St Helens for glass making. By 2018 the site had become a Highways Depot. (RailOnline)

113. On 12th April 1962, class 4F 0-6-0 no. 44393 approaches Congleton Lower Junction with a short freight from Brunswick Street, seen from the Macclesfield Canal aqueduct. In the left foreground is Lower Junction signal cabin and a locomotive watering point. The connecting line to Upper Junction goes off to the right. In the background the Congleton – Macclesfield main line runs across the picture; at left we see part of Congleton Viaduct, which has 10 arches and crosses Dane in Shaw Brook. (F.W.Shuttleworth)

BIDULPH

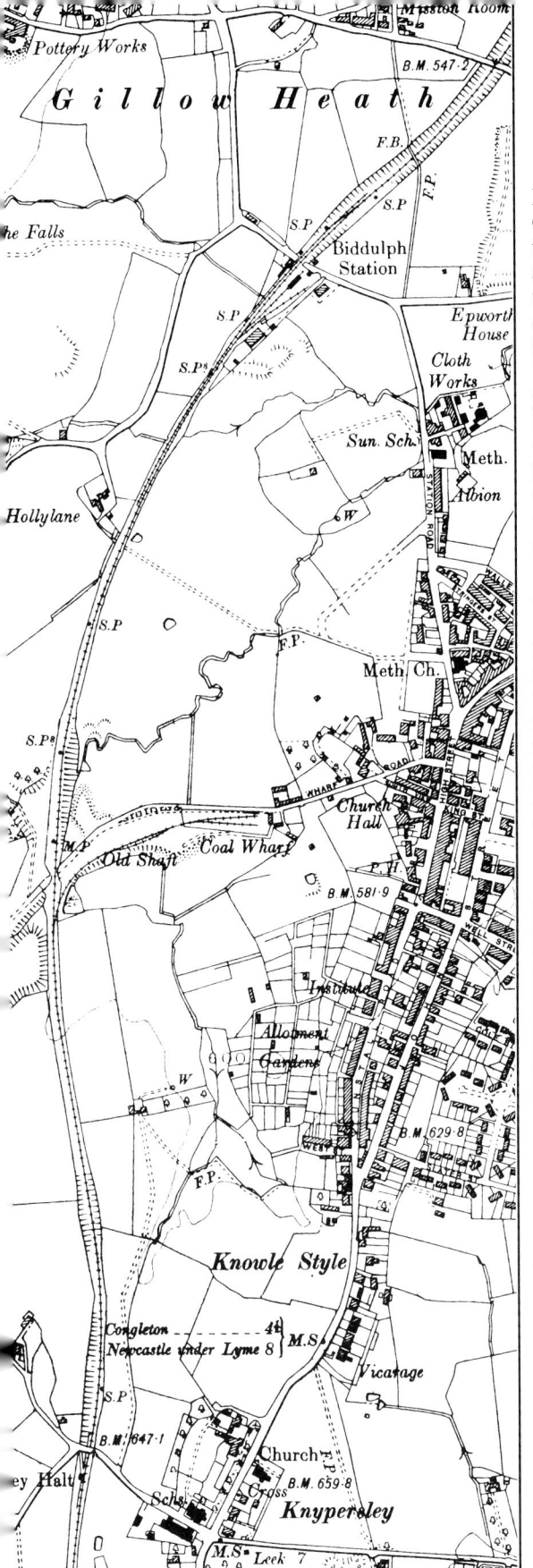

XXXVI. Biddulph was 2½ miles from Congleton Lower Junction, during which time the line crossed from Cheshire to Staffordshire and followed the course of Biddulph Brook upstream. There was a halt midway at Mossley, originally an unadvertised stop for miners, but in the public timetable between 1st October 1919 and 13th April 1925 when it closed. No photograph has come to light. The district of Biddulph was not created until 1894, prior to which the township was called Bradley Green. From its opening until 30th April 1897 the station was called Gillow Heath. The High Street was ½ mile uphill to the south east, and Biddulph Grange, noted for its landscaped gardens, was 1¼ miles north east. Knypersley Halt opened one mile south of Biddulph on 1st October 1914 and closed with the withdrawal of the passenger service from 11th July 1927. Again, no photographs have been handed down. This was close to the summit of the line at around 640 feet above sea level. The streams marked on the map drain to the River Mersey, whilst a quarter mile south of Knypersley cross roads is Trent Head Well, the source of the River Trent which drains to the Humber Estuary.

CONGLETON.

Distance from station, ¾ mile.
A telegraph station.
HOTEL.—Lion and Swan.
MARKET DAY.—Saturday.
FAIRS.—Thursday before Shrovetide, May 12th, July 12th, and Nov. 22nd.

A municipal borough and old town, with manufactures of silk and cotton. Population, 12,344. It is on the Dane, in the neighbourhood of the wild moorland country which borders Derbyshire and Staffordshire. Here may be seen several old timbered houses, large silk, cotton, and ribbon factories, town hall, and good grammar school. In the vicinity are *Eaton Hall*, G. Antrobus, Esq., and *Somerford Park*, Sir C. Shakerley, Bart. At *Biddulph* are the picturesque ruins of an Elizabethan house, destroyed in the civil wars. *Knypersley Hall*. Lime quarries are worked under the Mow Cop, a peak 1,091 feet high.

The route from Congleton to Macclesfield is rich in natural beauties, and furnishes various objects worthy attention, amongst which is a stupendous viaduct across the Dane valley.

Cloud-End and Mow Cop are noble features in the landscape to the right, between Macclesfield and the Potteries. Cloud-End is a bold promontory.

Bradshaw Guide, 1866.

114. This picture from 1912 shows the down side of the station at its zenith. At left is class D 0-6-0T no. 131, built at Stoke in 1891 and destined to last until the end of 1936, on a Stoke – Congleton passenger train. All of the modest station buildings are in view, as also are some staff and passers-by. The level crossing separates the station from the signal box, which was of a similar design by McKenzie & Holland to Congleton Station box, and which was in use from 1875 to 1931 when the line was singled, retaining the up line. Out of sight on the up side was a second platform, at the back of which was the goods shed which closed from 5th October 1964. After closure the passenger station became a private residence. (Biddulph Museum)

BLACK BULL

→ XXXVII. The locality was dominated by the ironworks and collieries of Robert Heath & Co, serving which was one of the main reasons for the construction of the Biddulph Valley branch. The site was connected to the NSR at Heath Junction, close to the top of the map, where double track from Stoke ended. The Biddulph Valley Ironworks commenced operations soon after the opening of the railway, using coal and ironstone mined on site. The works closed in 1928 in the face of bitter competition, but coal mining, concentrated on Victoria Pit, continued until 1982. The complex was also connected to Birchenwood (map XXXI), two miles away, by the mineral line passing Brown Lees Colliery, which closed in 1927. Black Bull station was just over one mile south of Knypersley. It took its name from an inn on the Newcastle to Congleton road at Brindley Ford. It was known as Black Bull Childerplay from 1873-86, then as Black Bull for Biddulph and Chell until 30th April 1897. It was further restyled as Black Bull Brindley Ford from October 1914 until the end of the NSR; the LMS listed it as, simply, Black Bull. The passenger station served throughout the 63 years of the train service, whilst goods facilities lasted until the start of 1964. Heath Junction to Ford Green closed entirely from 24th January 1976. The Union & U.D. Boundary separates Staffordshire from the County Borough of Stoke-on-Trent.

Map labels

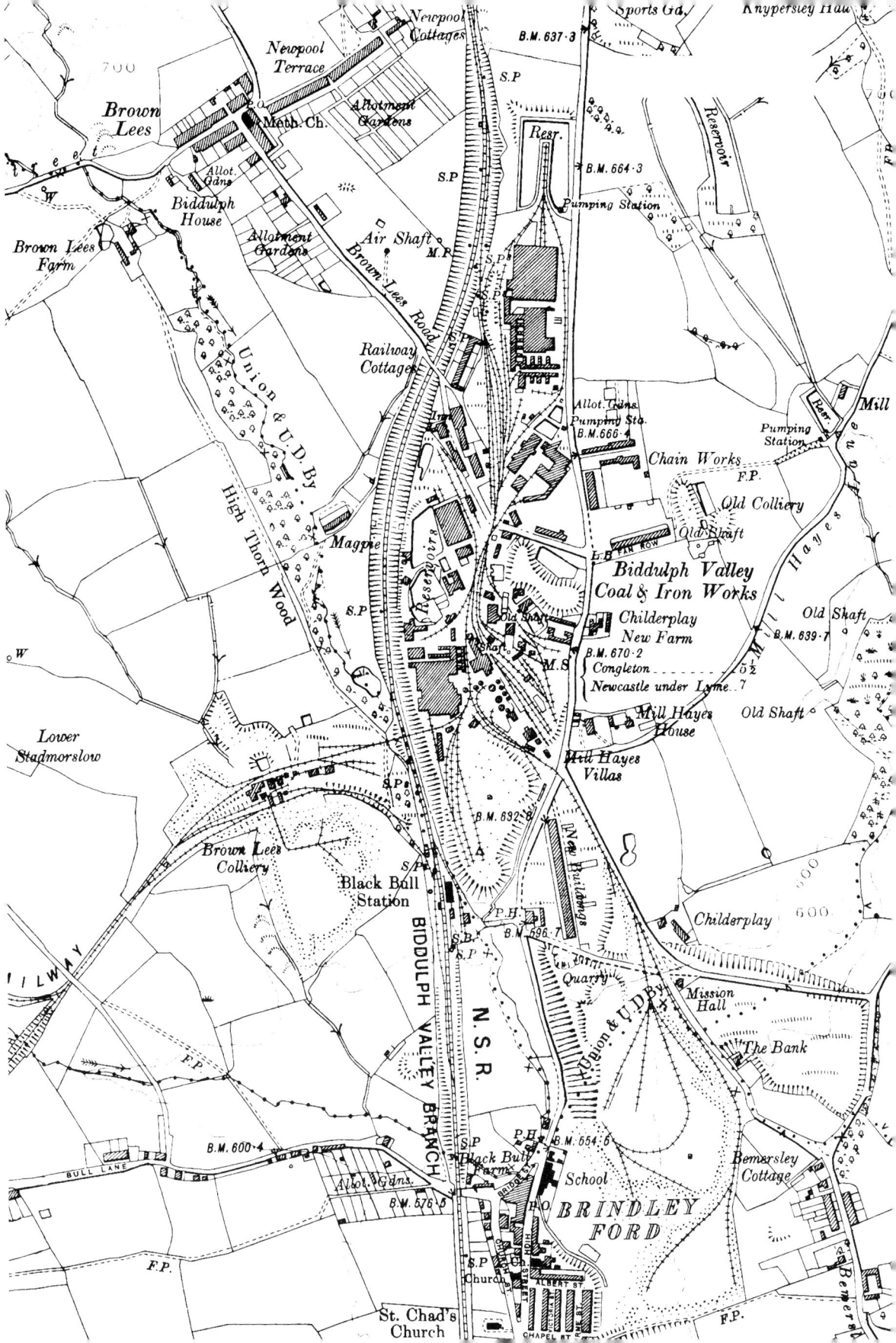

- Knypersley Hall
- Sports Gd
- B.M. 637·3
- Newpool Cottages
- Newpool Terrace
- Meth. Ch.
- BROWN LEES
- Allotment Gardens
- S.P
- Reservoir
- Resr.
- B.M. 664·3
- Pumping Station
- Allot. Gdns
- Biddulph House
- Allotment Gardens
- Air Shaft
- Brown Lees Farm
- Brown Lees Road
- S.P
- Railway Cottages
- Union & U.D. By
- High Thorp Wood
- Allot. Gdns
- Pumping Sta.
- B.M. 666·4
- Chain Works
- Pumping Station
- Resr
- Mill
- F.P.
- Old Colliery
- Magpie
- Old Shaft
- Reservoir
- S.P
- Old Shaft
- Biddulph Valley Coal & Iron Works
- Childerplay New Farm
- B.M. 670·2
- Congleton 5½
- Newcastle under Lyme 7
- Old Shaft
- B.M. 639·7
- Mill Hayes House
- Mill Hayes Villas
- Lower Stadmorslow
- W
- New Buildings
- B.M. 632·8
- Brown Lees Colliery
- Black Bull Station
- S.P
- P.H.
- B.M. 596·7
- S.P
- Childerplay
- 600
- Quarry
- Union & U.D. By
- Mission Hall
- The Bank
- RAILWAY
- BIDDULPH VALLEY BRANCH
- N.S.R.
- F.P.
- BULL LANE
- B.M. 600·4
- Allot. Gdns.
- B.M. 576·5
- P.H.
- B.M. 554·6
- Black Bull Farm
- School
- BRINDLEY FORD
- Bemersley Cottage
- F.P.
- S.P
- Church
- ALBERT ST.
- St. Chad's Church
- CHAPEL ST.

115. This north-facing view of the closed station dates from around 1948. On the left is a hopper for loading wagons with what appears to be granite ballast. The bridge in the background carried the Birchenwood line over the NSR, whilst the aerial ropeway carried spoil from Victoria Colliery to the site of Brown Lees for tipping. Note the end of a line of wagons at the colliery at a higher elevation than the NSR. Black Bull signal box stood behind the photographer. It had 26 levers and was in use between 1879 and 1967. (D.Thompson/R.Humm coll.)

116. Heaths built their own locomotives, 14 in all, between 1885 and 1925. Here we see one of them, fleet no. 16, an 0-6-0ST of 1924, passing Newchapel village with a short haul of coal from Victoria Colliery to Birchenwood on 9th April 1962. The line climbed to over 700ft above sea level, and the spark arrester perched on top of the chimney controlled the emission of burning cinders when working hard. This loco was in its last year of operation, and the line closed in 1965. (R.Hateley/RCTS)

SOUTH OF BLACK BULL: CHATTERLEY-WHITFIELD

→ 117. On 17th June 1990, 0-4-0ST no. 6 of Norton & Biddulph Collieries works a short demonstration freight. This locomotive has an interesting history. It was another of the Robert Heath & Co built locos, dating from 1886, and worked both at Victoria and Norton collieries, ending a long career (during which it was rebuilt at least twice) at the latter in 1969. It was claimed for preservation by Staffordshire County Council and was stored until transferred to Chatterley Whitfield in 1983. A further rebuild to working order followed before it was displayed at the National Garden Festival at Etruria in 1986. It was then based at Chatterley Whitfield until moving to the Foxfield Light Rly in April 1994. See also picture no. 85. (T.Heavyside)

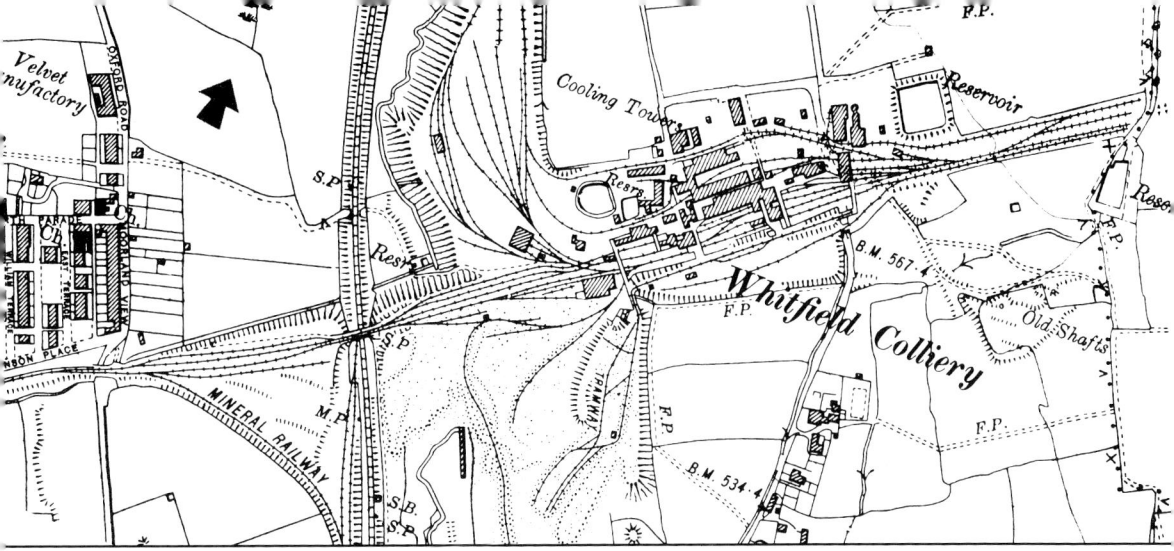

XXXVIII. Midway between Black Bull and Ford Green the NSR passed Whitfield Colliery to the east. This pre-dated the railway, to which it was initially connected. However, with much of the colliery's output being used by Chatterley Ironworks (map XVI), which was under common ownership, a private line was built in the 1870s which ran south westward, off the left-hand margin of this map, to Pinnox Junction (map XXIX) where it joined the NSR's Tunstall Branch to reach Longport. The business was renamed Chatterley-Whitfield Collieries Ltd in 1891, and the pit retained the double-barrelled name upon nationalisation. The private railway continued under NCB ownership until 1964, when the pit was linked once again to the Biddulph Valley line. The colliery closed in January 1976 when the last workings were linked to Wolstanton. The signal box marked at the foot of the map was Whitfield Siding, which had 20 levers and was in use from 1910 to 1962. Subsequently, the colliery became Chatterley Whitfield Mining Museum. It was possible to access underground workings until 1985 when the closure of Wolstanton ended ventilation, following which visitors could only descend a short distance. Visitor numbers declined, and the museum closed in August 1993. However, in 2018 the surface buildings survived intact as Britain's biggest remaining colliery site, and occasional open days were held.

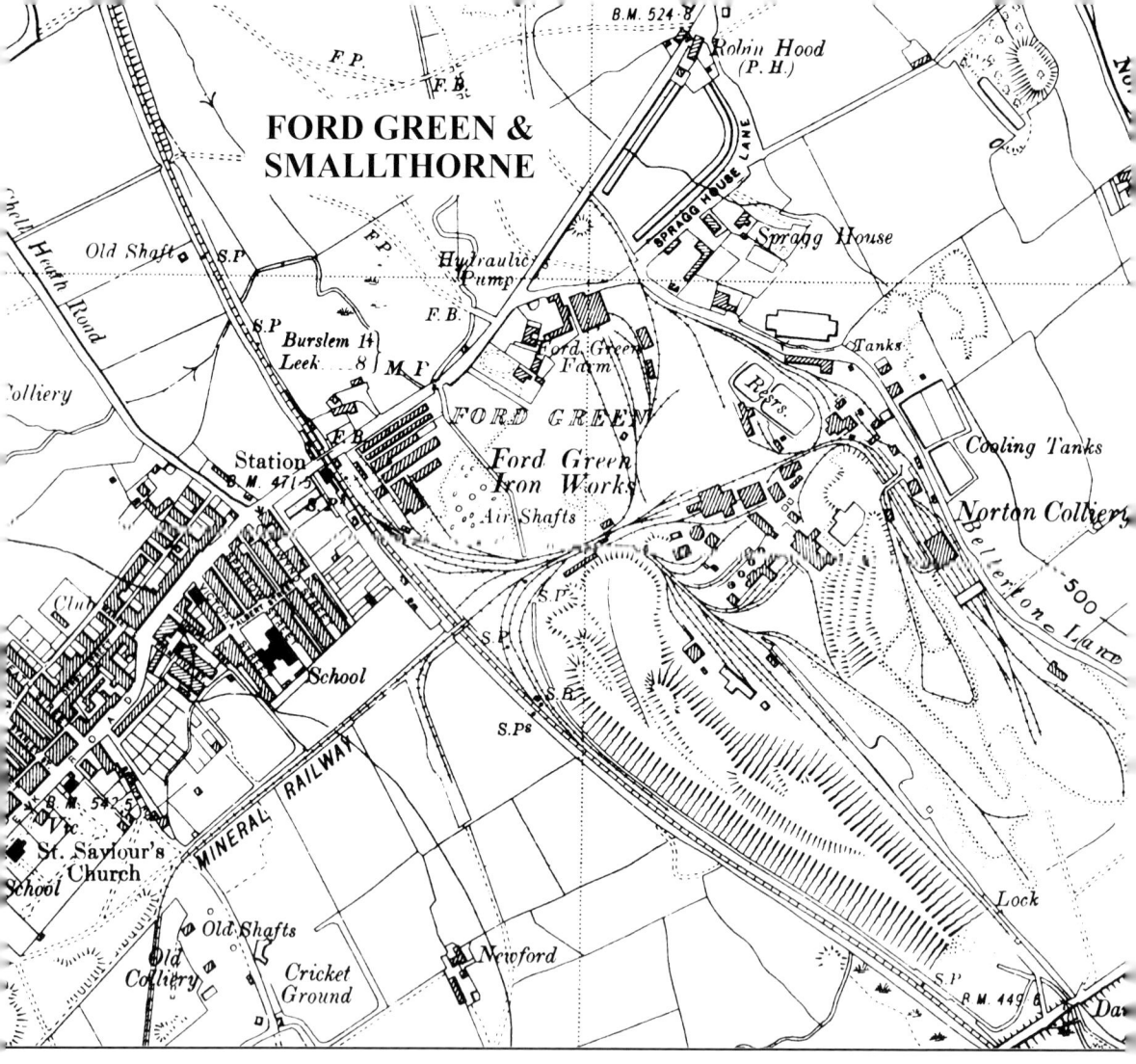

XXXIX. Ford Green was 2¾ miles from Black Bull. The suffix was added around 1887. It served throughout the duration of the passenger service and remained available for excursion traffic until August 1963. Goods facilities ended from 6th January 1964. Robert Heath & Co established the Ford Green Ironworks in the 1860s, and steel was also produced in later years. As with Biddulph Valley Ironworks, production ceased in 1928. Norton Colliery was on the site of old pit workings and lasted until June 1977; Ford Green to Milton Junction (map VIII) was then closed. This was the final section of the Biddulph Valley line and was a little less than one mile.

118. This undated view was from the footbridge, which was installed by the NSR in the 1890s. The line was busy at that time and the level crossing frequently closed to road traffic. The single storey station building is at the very northern end of the down platform, whilst the station masters house is at the opposite end. Beyond that is the goods shed, served by a single siding. The tall signal box dominates the down side, with the wheel controlling the crossing gates clearly visible. This box had a long working life, from 1887 to 1976.
(Railway Station Photographs)

119. This picture is dated 16th August 1958, a Saturday, and the evening shadows are lengthening as what is probably a return excursion approaches on the down line from the Biddulph direction. We can see that the platforms are staggered either side of the level crossing, and close inspection reveals there are two buses waiting for the train to pass. The conical spoil tip in the background was at Chatterley Whitfield. The end of the regular passenger service took effect on 11th July 1927. (R.Humm coll.)

120. On 3rd October 1960, 4F 0-6-0 no. 44386 is approaching the station heading north with empty coal wagons, probably bound for Victoria Colliery. The train is passing Ford Green Yard signal box, which controlled movements in and out of Norton Colliery. The bridge formerly carried a steeply graded colliery branch from Norton to pits at Holden Lane and Nettlebank, long closed by this time.
(A.Vaughan/J.Suter coll.)

MP Middleton Press

EVOLVING THE ULTIMATE RAIL ENCYCLOPEDIA

Easebourne Midhurst GU29 9AZ. Tel:01730 813169

www.middletonpress.co.uk email:info@middletonpress.co.uk

A-978 0 906520 B- 978 1 873793 C- 978 1 901706 D-978 1 904474

E - 978 1 906008 F - 978 1 908174 G - 978 1 910356

Our RAILWAY titles are listed below. Please check availability by looking at our website *middletonpress.co.uk*, telephoning us or by requesting a Brochure which includes our *LATEST* RAILWAY TITLES also our TRAMWAY, TROLLEYBUS, MILITARY and COASTAL series

A

Abergavenny to Merthyr C 91 8
Abertillery & Ebbw Vale Lines D 84 5
Aberystwyth to Carmarthen E 90 1
Allhallows - Branch Line to A 62 8
Alton - Branch Lines to A 11 6
Ambergate to Buxton G 28 9
Andover to Southampton A 82 6
Ascot - Branch Lines around A 64 2
Ashburton - Branch Line to B 95 4
Ashford - Steam to Eurostar B 67 1
Ashford to Dover A 48 2
Austrian Narrow Gauge D 04 3
Avonmouth - BL around D 42 5
Aylesbury to Rugby D 91 3

B

Baker Street to Uxbridge D 90 6
Bala to Llandudno E 87 1
Banbury to Birmingham D 27 2
Banbury to Cheltenham E 03 5
Bangor to Holyhead F 01 7
Bangor to Portmadoc E 72 7
Barking to Southend C 80 2
Barmouth to Pwllheli E 53 6
Barry - Branch Lines around D 50 0
Bartlow - Branch Lines to F 27 7
Basingstoke to Salisbury A 89 4
Bath Green Park to Bristol C 36 9
Bath to Evercreech Junction A 60 4
Beamish 40 years on rails E94 9
Bedford to Wellingborough D 31 9
Berwick to Drem F 64 2
Berwick to St. Boswells F 75 8
B'ham to Tamworth & Nuneaton F 63 5
Birkenhead to West Kirby F 61 1
Birmingham to Wolverhampton E253
Blackburn to Hellifield F 95 6
Bletchley to Cambridge D 94 4
Bletchley to Rugby E 07 9
Bodmin - Branch Lines around B 83 1
Boston to Lincoln F 80 2
Bournemouth to Evercreech Jn A 46 8
Bournemouth to Weymouth A 57 4
Bradshaw's History F18 5
Bradshaw's Rail Times 1850 F 13 0
Branch Lines series - see town names
Brecon to Neath D 43 2
Brecon to Newport D 16 6
Brecon to Newtown E 06 2
Brighton to Eastbourne A 16 1
Brighton to Worthing A 03 1
Bristol to Taunton D 03 6
Bromley South to Rochester B 23 7
Bromsgrove to Birmingham D 87 6
Bromsgrove to Gloucester D 73 9
Broxbourne to Cambridge F16 1
Brunel - A railtour D 74 6
Bude - Branch Line to B 29 9
Burnham to Evercreech Jn B 68 0

C

Cambridge to Ely D 55 5
Canterbury - BLs around B 58 9
Cardiff to Dowlais (Cae Harris) E 47 5
Cardiff to Pontypridd E 95 6
Cardiff to Swansea E 42 0
Carlisle to Hawick E 85 7
Carmarthen to Fishguard E 66 6
Caterham & Tattenham Corner B251
Central & Southern Spain NG E 91 8
Chard and Yeovil - BLs a C 30 7
Charing Cross to Dartford A 75 8
Charing Cross to Orpington A 96 3
Cheddar - Branch Line to B 90 9
Cheltenham to Andover C 43 7
Cheltenham to Redditch D 81 4
Chesterfield to Lincoln G 21 0
Chester to Birkenhead F 21 5
Chester to Manchester F 51 2
Chester to Rhyl E 93 2
Chester to Warrington F 40 6
Chichester to Portsmouth A 14 7
Clacton and Walton - BLs to F 04 8
Clapham Jn to Beckenham Jn B 36 7
Cleobury Mortimer - BLs a E 18 5
Clevedon & Portishead - BLs to D180
Consett to South Shields E 57 4
Cornwall Narrow Gauge D 56 2
Corris and Vale of Rheidol E 65 9
Coventry to Leicester G 00 5
Craven Arms to Llandeilo E 35 2
Craven Arms to Wellington E 33 8
Crawley to Littlehampton A 34 5
Crewe to Manchester F 57 4
Crewe to Wigan G 12 8
Cromer - Branch Lines around C 26 0
Croydon to East Grinstead B 48 0
Crystal Palace & Catford Loop B 87 1
Cyprus Narrow Gauge E 13 0

D

Darjeeling Revisited F 09 3
Darlington Leamside Newcastle E 28 4
Darlington to Newcastle D 98 2
Dartford to Sittingbourne B 34 3
Denbigh - Branch Lines around F 32 1
Derby to Chesterfield G 11 1
Derby to Stoke-on-Trent F 93 2
Derwent Valley - BL to the D 06 7
Devon Narrow Gauge E 09 3
Didcot to Banbury D 02 9
Didcot to Swindon C 84 0
Didcot to Winchester C 13 0
Diss to Norwich G 22 7
Dorset & Somerset NG D 76 0
Douglas - Laxey - Ramsey E 75 8
Douglas to Peel C 88 8
Douglas to Port Erin C 55 0
Douglas to Ramsey D 39 5
Dover to Ramsgate A 78 9
Drem to Edinburgh G 06 7
Dublin Northwards in 1950s E 31 4
Dunstable - Branch Lines to E 27 7

E

Ealing to Slough C 42 0
Eastbourne to Hastings A 27 7
East Cornwall Mineral Railways D 22 7
East Croydon to Three Bridges A 53 6
Eastern Spain Narrow Gauge E 56 7
East Grinstead - BLs to A 07 9
East Kent Light Railway A 61 1
East London - Branch Lines of C 44 4
East London Line B 80 0
East of Norwich - Branch Lines E 69 7
Effingham Junction - BLs a A 74 1
Ely to Norwich C 90 1
Enfield Town & Palace Gates D 32 6
Epsom to Horsham A 30 7
Eritrean Narrow Gauge E 38 3
Euston to Harrow & Wealdstone C 89 5
Exeter to Barnstaple B 15 2
Exeter to Newton Abbot C 49 9
Exeter to Tavistock B 69 5
Exmouth - Branch Lines to B 00 8

F

Fairford - Branch Line to A 52 9
Falmouth, Helston & St. Ives C 74 1
Fareham to Salisbury A 67 3
Faversham to Dover B 05 3
Felixstowe & Aldeburgh - BL to D 20 3
Fenchurch Street to Barking C 20 8
Festiniog - 50 yrs of enterprise C 83 3
Festiniog 1946-55 E 01 7
Festiniog in the Fifties B 68 8
Festiniog in the Sixties B 91 6
Ffestiniog in Colour 1955-82 F 25 3
Finsbury Park to Alexandra Pal C 02 8
French Metre Gauge Survivors F 88 8
Frome to Bristol B 77 0

G

Gainsborough to Sheffield G 17 3
Galashiels to Edinburgh F 52 9
Gloucester to Bristol D 35 7
Gloucester to Cardiff D 66 1
Gosport - Branch Lines around A 36 9
Greece Narrow Gauge D 72 2
Guildford to Redhill A 63 5

H

Hampshire Narrow Gauge D 36 4
Harrow to Watford D 14 2
Harwich & Hadleigh - BLs to F 02 4
Harz Revisited F 62 8
Hastings to Ashford A 37 6
Hawick to Galashiels F 36 9
Hawkhurst - Branch Line to A 66 6
Hayling - Branch Line to A 12 3
Hay-on-Wye - BL around D 92 0
Haywards Heath to Seaford A 28 4
Hemel Hempstead - BLs to D 88 3
Henley, Windsor & Marlow - BLa C77 2
Hereford to Newport D 54 8
Hertford & Hatfield - BLs a E 58 1
Hertford Loop E 71 0
Hexham to Carlisle D 75 3
Hexham to Hawick F 08 6
Hitchin to Peterborough D 07 4
Holborn Viaduct to Lewisham A 81 9
Horsham - Branch Lines to A 02 4
Hull, Hornsea and Withernsea G 27 2
Huntingdon - Branch Line to A 93 2

I

Ilford to Shenfield C 97 0
Ilfracombe - Branch Line to B 21 3
Ilkeston to Chesterfield G 26 5
Ipswich to Diss F 81 9
Ipswich to Saxmundham C 41 3
Isle of Man Railway Journey F 94 9
Isle of Wight Lines - 50 yrs C 12 3
Italy Narrow Gauge F 17 8

K

Kent Narrow Gauge C 45 1
Kettering to Nottingham F 82-6
Kidderminster to Shrewsbury E 10 9
Kingsbridge - Branch Line to C 98 7
Kings Cross to Potters Bar E 62 8
King's Lynn to Hunstanton F 58 1
Kingston & Hounslow Loops A 83 3
Kingswear - Branch Line to C 17 8

L

Lambourn - Branch Line to C 70 3
Launceston & Princetown - BLs C 19 2
Leek - Branch Line From G 01 2
Leicester to Burton F 85 7
Leicester to Nottingham G 15 9
Lewisham to Dartford A 92 5
Lincoln to Cleethorpes F 56 7
Lincoln to Doncaster G 03 6
Lines around Stamford F 98 7
Lines around Wimbledon B 75 6
Lines North of Stoke G 29 6
Liverpool Street to Chingford D 01 2
Liverpool Street to Ilford C 34 5
Llandeilo to Swansea E 46 8
London Bridge to Addiscombe B 20 6
London Bridge to East Croydon A 58 1
Longmoor - Branch Lines to A 41 3
Looe - Branch Line to C 22 2
Loughborough to Ilkeston G 24 1
Loughborough to Nottingham F 68 0
Lowestoft - BLs around E 40 6
Ludlow to Hereford E 14 7
Lydney - Branch Lines around E 26 0
Lyme Regis - Branch Line to A 45 1
Lynton - Branch Line to B 04 6

M

Machynlleth to Barmouth E 54 3
Maesteg and Tondu Lines F 06 2
Majorca & Corsica Narrow Gauge F 41 3
Mansfield to Doncaster G 23 4
March - Branch Lines around B 09 1
Market Drayton - BLs around F 67 3
Market Harborough to Newark F 86 4
Marylebone to Rickmansworth D 49 4
Melton Constable to Yarmouth Bch E031
Midhurst - Branch Lines of E 78 9
Midhurst - Branch Lines to F 00 0
Minehead - Branch Line to A 80 2
Mitcham Junction Lines B 01 5
Monmouth - Branch Lines to E 20 8
Monmouthshire Eastern Valleys D 71 5
Moretonhampstead - BL to C 27 7
Moreton-in-Marsh to Worcester D 26 5
Morpeth to Bellingham F 87 1
Mountain Ash to Neath D 80 7

N

Newark to Doncaster F 78 9
Newbury to Westbury C 66 6
Newcastle to Hexham D 69 2
Newport (IOW) - Branch Lines to A 26 0
Newquay - Branch Lines to C 71 0
Newton Abbot to Plymouth C 60 4
Newtown to Aberystwyth E 41 3
Northampton to Peterborough F 92 5
North East German NG D 44 9
Northern Alpine Narrow Gauge F 37 6
Northern France Narrow Gauge C 75 8
Northern Spain Narrow Gauge E 83 3
North London Line B 94 7
North of Birmingham F 55 0
North of Grimsby - Branch Lines G 09 8
North Woolwich - BLs around C 65 9
Nottingham to Boston F 70 3
Nottingham to Lincoln F 43 7
Nuneaton to Loughborough G 08 1

O

Ongar - Branch Line to E 05 5
Orpington to Tonbridge B 03 9
Oswestry - Branch Lines around E 60 4
Oswestry to Whitchurch E 81 9
Oxford to Bletchley D 57 9
Oxford to Moreton-in-Marsh D 15 9

P

Paddington to Ealing C 37 6
Paddington to Princes Risborough C819
Padstow - Branch Line to B 54 1
Peebles Loop G 19 7
Pembroke and Cardigan - BLs to F 20 1
Peterborough to Kings Lynn E 32 1
Peterborough to Lincoln F 89 5
Peterborough to Newark F 72 7
Plymouth - BLs around B 98 5
Plymouth to St. Austell C 63 5
Pontypool to Mountain Ash D 65 4
Pontypridd to Merthyr F 14 7
Pontypridd to Port Talbot E 86 4
Porthmadog 1954-94 - BLa B 31 2
Portmadoc 1923-46 - BLa B 13 8
Portsmouth to Southampton A 31 4
Portugal Narrow Gauge E 67 3
Potters Bar to Cambridge D 70 8
Preston to Blackpool G 16 6
Princes Risborough - BL to D 05 0
Princes Risborough to Banbury C 85 7

R

Railways to Victory C 16 1
Reading to Basingstoke B 27 5
Reading to Didcot C 79 6
Reading to Guildford A 47 5
Redhill to Ashford A 73 4
Return to Blaenau 1970-82 C 64 2
Rhyl to Bangor F 15 4
Rhymney & New Tredegar Lines E 48 2
Rickmansworth to Aylesbury D 61 6
Romania & Bulgaria NG E 23 9
Romneyrail C 32 1
Ross-on-Wye - BLs around E 30 7
Ruabon to Barmouth E 84 0
Rugby to Birmingham E 37 6
Rugby to Loughborough F 12 3
Rugby to Stafford F 07 9
Rugeley to Stoke-on-Trent F 90 1
Ryde to Ventnor A 19 2

S

Salisbury to Westbury B 39 8
Salisbury to Yeovil B 06 0
Sardinia and Sicily Narrow Gauge F 50 5
Saxmundham to Yarmouth C 69 7
Saxony & Baltic Germany Revisited F 71 0
Saxony Narrow Gauge D 47 0
Seaton & Sidmouth - BLs to A 95 6
Selsey - Branch Line to A 04 8
Sheerness - Branch Line to B 16 2
Sheffield towards Manchester G 18 0
Shenfield to Ipswich E 96 3
Shrewsbury - Branch Line to A 86 4
Shrewsbury to Chester E 70 3
Shrewsbury to Crewe F 48 2
Shrewsbury to Ludlow E 21 5
Shrewsbury to Newtown E 29 1
Sierra Leone Narrow Gauge D 28 9
Sirhowy Valley Line E 12 3
Sittingbourne to Ramsgate A 90 1
Skegness & Mablethorpe - BL to F 84 0
Slough to Newbury C 56 7
South African Two-foot gauge E 51 2
Southampton to Bournemouth A 42 0
Southend & Southminster BLs E 76 5
Southern Alpine Narrow Gauge F 22 2
Southern France Narrow Gauge C 47 5
South London Line B 46 6
South Lynn to Norwich City F 03 1
Southwold - Branch Line to A 15 4
Spalding - Branch Lines around E 5
Spalding to Grimsby F 65 9 6
Stafford to Chester F 34 5
Stafford to Wellington F 59 8
St Albans to Bedford D 08 1
St. Austell to Penzance C 67 3
St. Boswell to Berwick F 44 4
Steaming Through Isle of Wight A 5
Stourbridge to Wolverhampton E 16
St. Pancras to Barking D 68 5
St. Pancras to Folkestone E 88 8
St. Pancras to St. Albans C 78 9
Stratford to Cheshunt F 53 6
Stratford-u-Avon to Birmingham D 7
Stratford-u-Avon to Cheltenham C 2
Sudbury - Branch Lines to F 19 2
Surrey Narrow Gauge C 87 1
Sussex Narrow Gauge C 68 0
Swaffham - Branch Lines around F
Swanage to 1999 - BL to A 33 8
Swanley to Ashford B 45 9
Swansea - Branch Lines around F 3
Swansea to Carmarthen E 59 8
Swindon to Bristol C 96 3
Swindon to Gloucester D 46 3
Swindon to Newport D 30 2
Swiss Narrow Gauge C 94 9

T

Talyllyn 60 E 98 7
Tamworth to Derby F 76 5
Taunton to Barnstaple B 60 2
Taunton to Exeter C 82 6
Taunton to Minehead F 39 0
Tavistock to Plymouth B 88 6
Tenterden - Branch Line to A 21 5
Three Bridges to Brighton A 35 2
Tilbury Loop C 86 4
Tiverton - BLs around C 62 8
Tivetshall to Beccles D 41 8
Tonbridge to Hastings A 44 4
Torrington - Branch Lines to B 37 4
Tourist Railways of France G 04 3
Towcester - BLs around E 39 0
Tunbridge Wells BLs A 32 1

U

Upwell - Branch Line to B 64 0
Uttoxeter to Macclesfield G 05 0

V

Victoria to Bromley South A 98 7
Victoria to East Croydon A 40 6
Vivarais Revisited E 08 6

W

Walsall Routes F 45 1
Wantage - Branch Line to D 25 8
Wareham to Swanage 50 yrs D 09
Waterloo to Windsor A 54 3
Waterloo to Woking A 38 3
Watford to Leighton Buzzard D 45 6
Wellingborough to Leicester F 73 4
Welshpool to Llanfair E 49 9
Wenford Bridge to Fowey C 09 3
Westbury to Bath B 55 8
Westbury to Taunton C 76 5
West Cornwall Mineral Rlys D 48 7
West Croydon to Epsom B 08 4
West German Narrow Gauge D 93 7
West London - BLs of C 50 5
West London Line B 84 8
West Wiltshire - BLs of D 12 8
Weymouth - BLs A 65 9
Willesden Jn to Richmond B 71 8
Wimbledon to Beckenham C 58 1
Wimbledon to Epsom B 62 6
Wimborne - BLs around A 97 0
Wirksworth - Branch Lines to G 10
Wisbech - BLs around C 01 7
Witham & Kelvedon - BLs a E 82 6
Woking to Alton A 59 8
Woking to Portsmouth A 25 3
Woking to Southampton A 55 0
Wolverhampton to Shrewsbury E 4
Wolverhampton to Stafford F 79 6
Worcester to Birmingham D 97 5
Worcester to Hereford D 38 8
Worthing to Chichester A 06 2
Wrexham to New Brighton F 47 5
Wroxham - BLs around F 31 4

Y

Yeovil - 50 yrs change C 38 3
Yeovil to Dorchester A 76 5
Yeovil to Exeter A 91 8
York to Scarborough F 23 9